CULTURE SHOCK!

Argentina

Fiona Adams

D0257068

·K·U·P·E·R·A·R·D·

In the same series

Argentina	Germany	Mauritius	Sweden
Australia	Greece	Mexico	Switzerland
Bolivia	Hong Kong	Morocco	Syria
Britain	India	Myanmar	Taiwan
California	Indonesia	Nepal	Thailand
Canada	Iran	Netherlands	Turkey
Chile	Ireland	Norway	UAE
China	Israel	Pakistan	Ukraine
Cuba	Italy	Philippines	USA
Czech Republic	Japan	Singapore	USA—The South
Denmark	Korea	South Africa	Venezuela
Egypt	Laos	Spain	Vietnam
France	Malaysia	Sri Lanka	

A Student's Guide
A Traveller's Medical Guide
Living & Working in Chicago
Living & Working in London
Living & Working in New York
Living & Working in Paris
Living & Working in Rome

Living and Working Abroad—
  A Practical Guide
Living and Working Abroad—
  A Parent's Guide
Living and Working Abroad—
  A Wife's Guide

Culture Shock! Argentina
First published in Great Britain 2000 by
Kuperard
311 Ballards Lane
Finchley
London N12 8LY
Tel: 0208 446 2440 Fax: 0208 446 2441
Email: kuperard@bravo.clara.net

Kuperard is an imprint of Bravo Ltd.

Illustrations by TRIGG

Printed in Singapore

ISBN 1-85733-253-9

To Jean and Roger,
with love

CONTENTS

Introduction *7*

Acknowledgments *11*

1 The Historical Setting *13*

2 The Country *33*

3 The People *50*

4 Social Customs *79*

5 Business Customs *109*

6 Food and Drink *125*

7 Football and Other Religions *148*

8 Language *171*

9 Survival Skills *191*

10 Strategic Directory *228*

Cultural Quiz *239*

Further Reading *244*

About the Author *249*

Index *250*

INTRODUCTION

Argentina has always been the odd one out in South America. Taking up practically the entire bottom half of that continent, it is second in size only to Brazil. It includes territories as diverse as the frozen wastes of Tierra del Fuego, the fertile plains of the pampas, subtropical rainforest and the sweeping Atlantic coastline. But it's the people and not just the fabulous geography that makes Argentina such an extraordinary country.

If you choose to stay or seek your fortune in Argentina, you won't be alone. The country is a nation of immigrants who have generated a fiery blend of European sophistication and Latin passion in the heart of South America. The happy result of this blend is that everyone has brought along their own slice of culture, be it dashing British polo or divine Italian pizza. Yet at the same time something unique has emerged in Argentina. You can hear it in the fast *lunfardo* slang spoken on the streets of Buenos Aires, you can see it in the erotic embrace of the tango dancers and you can taste it in the mouth-watering steaks.

By the time your taxi driver picks you up from Ezeiza airport and weaves through a terrifying maze of traffic lanes with his foot firmly glued to the accelerator, you start to get some idea of what you've let yourself in for. He is gesticulating wildly – hands waving this way and that like so many windmills – and letting loose a stream of Spanish. It's hard to follow exactly what he is saying as his sentences are peppered with *lunfardo*. He sounds almost Italian but you manage to pick up something about Argentina having the best-looking people, the finest beef, the greatest footballers and basically being the best place in the world.

So maybe their international reputation for arrogance is well deserved. But when you come to think of it, the Argentines have an awful lot to be arrogant about. Good looks aside, Argentina can boast a share of the world's most spectacular waterfall, the highest mountain this side of the Himalayas and one of the most sophisticated cities on earth. Culturally, it's a dream and continues to churn out writers of extraordinary calibre, cutting-edge cinema, lively theatre and of course the tango. There aren't many other dances in the world that can make the bold claim of being 'the closest thing you'll find to a vertical expression of horizontal desire'.

Argentines are a boisterous lot. If you enjoy being the centre of attention you're in for considerable competition. In the cities, there is a constant background noise of revving engines, screeching brakes, televised football matches and the happy clatter of packed restaurants. This is a country that *loves* to talk and will do so loudly at every available opportunity. Spontaneous debates spring up on street corners,

Photo: Jamie Grant

Ooh, so sensual, so steamy! Tango pros show us how to do it the right way.

in bank queues and on buses. Eavesdroppers will be in heaven. They can sit on one side of a leafy plaza and happily listen in on a conversation on the other side.

In Argentina you go out at all hours and you go out to be seen. It is not unusual to finish dinner at midnight or grab breakfast on your way back from an exhausting night on the tiles before heading straight to work. Argentines are certainly not wallflowers, and they won't expect you to be one either. But if you really want to get the most out of your stay in Argentina, you may have to revamp your sleeping habits. This is the perfect place for insomniacs. Whether it's the result of an unrivalled caffeine intake, the simple fact that they can never pass up an opportunity to socialise or sheer willpower alone, Argentines seem to spend less time asleep than other nationalities.

This is also the land of svelte models and ravishing polo players so come fashionably prepared. They are a sophisticated bunch and Buenos Aires has put in a lot of hard work to be known as the Paris of South America. Life in the countryside may be more relaxed and a welcome respite from the frantic city pace, but even here things are done with style.

You have also chosen a relatively safe country, provided you don't get inside a car (Argentines are some of the most aggressive drivers in the world). Forget any preconceived notions about South America. Down here you can eat the salad *and* drink the tap water. People still walk around the streets at three in the morning – actually they're probably just on their way out. There are no really nasty bugs, few terrorist attacks and even the generals – a key feature in the country's political history – have taken a back seat since the return to democracy in 1983.

Despite its enormous size and European feel, Argentina retains a remarkably intimate atmosphere. Argentines are the most courteous of people and you will always find yourself drawn into conversation. It can be safely said that wherever you come from in the world, no one will raise an eyebrow or call you a *gringo* straight off. If you're really lucky you may even be stopped and asked directions.

Packed with practical tips, invaluable information and amusing anecdotes, the following pages will take you through the intricacies of Argentine society and customs and will make your stay all the more enjoyable.

So take a deep breath because coming to Argentina is like being sucked into the movies with the volume turned up full. Larger-than-life characters frolic through unbelievable scenery, everyone drives at 100 miles an hour and the weekend starts on Wednesday.

ACKNOWLEDGMENTS

My special thanks go to Jamie Grant for the wonderful photos, also Rodolfo 'Yoyo' de Los Santos, Nico Busch, Santi Norris and Daniela Volker for patiently helping me with hours of research. Thanks as well to Charlie Froggatt for his insights on polo and Katya Lamerton Viegas for long discussions on the tango. I'd also like to thank the 'gang' in San Telmo – Uri, Anim, Diego, Fernando, Chino, Shannen and DJ – for being such lovely flatmates; Federico and Veronica D'Angelo in Ushuaia; Mark Cramer, Dan Buck, Dereck Foster, Richard Cunningham, Joe Oppenheimer and my parents, Jean and Roger, for their support and encouragement. And finally, many thanks to the hundreds of others who have helped along the way and without whom this book would not have been possible.

ARGENTINA

Chapter One

THE HISTORICAL SETTING

'I must tell you there's scarcely a gaucho left
All round my native parts;
Some are under the grass, and some have fled,
And some in the frontier wars are dead;
For as soon, in this land, as one war is done,
Some other rumpus starts.'

—from *The Gaucho Martín Fierro*
by José Hernández,
translation by Walter Owen

The first thing that strikes the foreign visitor to Argentina is whether the Argentines are Latin Americans or Europeans who through a strange twist of fate have been uprooted and thrown into the middle of South America. It is a dilemma that continues to confound the Argentines themselves.

A local saying reasons that 'Argentina is the most European of the Latin American nations because its people are from the most Latin of the European nations'. It's certainly true that the vast majority of the population can trace their forefathers back to Europe (mainly Spain and Italy). And Buenos Aires appears to be a city built by some seriously homesick Europeans. A short walk across this most sophisticated metropolis is like a whirlwind tour of Europe. The wide, sweeping boulevards, expansive parks and striking architecture are more in tune with London, Paris or Madrid than other Latin American cities. Glance at the menus in the city's numerous restaurants and you could think you're in Italy. Mingle with the polo players and you could be in Britain. Go shopping and you might think you're in France. Culturally and emotionally, Argentina remains firmly attached to Europe and its eyes are continually straining across the Atlantic for inspiration and approval.

Occasionally, as the distance from their ideological homeland makes itself felt, the Argentines sink into despair and moan that they feel abandoned by the rest of the world. They say that *porteños*, as the inhabitants of Buenos Aires are better known, are a melancholic lot. Maybe it's the thought of an exile without return – a creeping nostalgia for the countries that they have left behind.

But once you get out of the major cities there is a dramatic return to South American reality. Horse-drawn carts piled with exotic fruits rattle over cobbled streets and men in ponchos and sombreros slip away from the midday heat for long siestas. Ah, you decide, maybe I'm in South America after all. Then an expensive-looking blonde in a fur coat strides past and you're back to square one.

This perplexing reality is largely a result of Argentina's unique history, which saw an enormous country bereft of its original Indian inhabitants and the space taken over by millions of European immigrants and their dreams.

SHAKY BEGINNINGS

The Conquistadors, finding no silver or gold in the region that was to become present-day Argentina, nor local indigenous tribes docile enough to exploit, pretty much left the place to its own devices, preferring instead to plunder the great Indian empires of Central America and Peru. By 1570, less than 2,000 Spaniards lived in the country and Buenos Aires itself was little more than an abandoned settlement.

Today's common expression that *Buenos Aires te mata* (Buenos Aires kills you) – a jokey reference to the oppressive heaving metropolis of 12 million inhabitants and stifling humidity – actually has some historical grains of truth; the earliest visitors to the region didn't fare well to say the least. The first European to explore the River Plate in 1516, Juan Diaz de Solis, a Portuguese navigator employed by the Spanish Crown, was attacked and, legend has it, eaten by the local Querandí Indians. Some 20 years later the aristocrat Pedro de Mendoza set sail from Spain and founded a small encampment which he christened Santa Maria de Buen Aire after the patron saint of sailors. Besieged by Indians, Mendoza's 1,600-strong army at one stage resorted to eating the leather off their shoes to avoid starvation. One Spaniard reputedly ate his own brother. By 1541, the settlement was abandoned. Mendoza managed to escape Buenos Aires alive, only to perish of syphilis on the high seas. Meanwhile, some of the livestock which had been brought over by the Spaniards escaped and were left to run wild on the fertile pampas where they bred rapidly. They would soon become the criollo ponies and enormous cattle herds that made Argentina so famous.

It wasn't until 1580 before another Spaniard, Juan de Garay, tried his luck in Buenos Aires. He planted a tree and drew up a plan for the

Colonial church and plaza in the village of Cachi, province of Salta.

city before being caught unawares by Indians as he took a siesta on the banks of the Río de La Plata. The Querandí killed Garay, but this time Buenos Aires survived – an isolated outpost on the fringe of the Spanish empire.

Other Argentine cities including Tucumán, Salta, Jujuy, La Rioja and Córdoba were colonised from the north, by way of Potosi in Alto Peru (present-day Bolivia) and Lima, where the Spanish Crown had its viceroyalty. Many beautiful colonial buildings and churches survive intact around central plazas, making such cities some of the most picturesque in the country. Their cobbled streets, arranged in a neat grid-like system, make orientation a dream.

Back in Buenos Aires, the local population indulged in a profit-able smuggling racket with the Portuguese and British – much to the irritation of the Spanish Crown who insisted that all trade went via their viceroyalty in Lima, Peru. They also traded in the hides and meat of the enormous herds of cattle that roamed the pampas, the vast grassy plains that surround Buenos Aires. It was at this time that the legendary gaucho first emerged. Argentina's cowboy began his life as a cattle hustler and an outlaw during the 18th and 19th centuries, fearlessly riding across the pampas on horseback.

It wasn't until 1776, nearly two hundred years after Garay's historic founding of Buenos Aires, that Argentina was finally given its own viceroyalty of the Río de la Plata with its seat in Buenos Aires.

So much for great beginnings. But if Argentina doesn't stand out like Peru or Mexico for the grandeur of its colonial days, it did produce more than its fair share of heroes when the criollos (Spaniards born in Argentina) finally shook off the Spanish Crown at the beginning of the 19th century.

BOOTING OUT THE SPANISH

A number of simultaneous events led to Spain's demise in the Americas, among them the Napoleonic wars in Europe and the increasing discontent of the criollos with their Spanish overlords and their infuriating trade laws. In Argentina, things were speeded along by a rather singular event.

In 1806, a reckless Englishman, Sir Home Popham, decided to invade Buenos Aires completely off his own bat. Popham, presumably still fired up after fighting the Dutch in Cape Town, had neither backing nor authorisation from the British government when he landed in Buenos Aires with a naval and military force of 1,600 men. Rather than standing his ground, the cowardly Spanish viceroy scuttled off to Córdoba, leaving the *porteños* to defend their city, which they did successfully. They ousted the British – not once, but again a year later, when the British government had decided that Popham was onto a good thing and sent a second expedition headed by Lieutenant General John Whitelocke. This unprecedented success boosted *porteño* self-esteem to such an extent that it gave them the added confidence to throw off their Spanish rulers in the revolution of 25 May 1810 and declare an independent junta.

Independence from Spain was formally proclaimed six years later on 9 July 1816 in the northern city of Tucumán. As a result, Argentina happily enjoys two more public holidays: both 25 May and 9 July are celebrated as national holidays. And both are among Buenos Aires' greatest landmarks. The Plaza de Mayo in front of the Casa Rosada (the presidential palace) commemorates the May Revolution and the giant road bisecting the city and arguably the widest road in the world is christened the Avenida Nueve de Julio (9th of July Avenue).

The real hero of the independence movement was General José de San Martín, the Argentine who went on to cross the Andes on horseback to liberate Chile and later Peru for good measure. He is one of the few historical figures who is above criticism in Argentina, and the anniversary of his death on August 17 is another national holiday. In almost every town and city in Argentina you will come across a street or plaza named after San Martín, and there is usually also a statue of the hero mounted on a rearing horse.

Independence from the Spanish Crown, however, didn't mean political stability for Argentina. The country remained wracked by political divisions, as provincial warlords competed for control. The most alarming development was the ever-widening chasm between the *porteños* of Buenos Aires and the rest of the country.

THE GREAT DIVIDE: BUENOS AIRES AND THE INTERIOR

If a *porteño* tells you that he comes from the north, what he probably means is that he's from the north of Buenos Aires city. The inhabitants of Buenos Aires are enormously proud of their city and at times are apt to believe it is the centre of the universe. The rest of Argentina is simply referred to as 'the Interior' – a somewhat murky and ill-defined description that embraces every possible terrain from Tierra del Fuego in the south to the dusty Bolivian border in the north.

While *porteños* tend to think of themselves as sophisticated creatures, they look upon their fellow countrymen from the Interior as something more akin to country yokels. It's a striking division between Buenos Aires and the Interior, one that can be traced back to the years just after independence when the country fell into two distinct camps – Unitarists and Federalists – and civil war ensued. The Unitarists, generally cosmopolitan city folk from Buenos Aires with eyes locked lovingly on Europe, believed in a strong central government (in Buenos Aires, of course). The Federalists wanted to preserve local autonomy and soon fell under the tyrannical rule of Juan Manuel de Rosas, the greatest Federalist of them all. (His portrait appears today, rather controversially, on the 20 peso bill. He is easily identifiable by his cruel looking mouth and enormous sideburns.)

Rosas, the gaucho warlord of Buenos Aires province, sought and achieved full dictatorial powers in 1829 and ran the province as he would a vast ranch. When his first term as governor ended, he left Buenos Aires on a military campaign to wipe out bands of Indians in the south, only to return to office in 1835 and rule for another 17 years with the help of an intricate spy network and brutal secret police. During Rosas' reign, you could get into trouble if you didn't wear a red ribbon – the federalist colour   or begin a letter with the slogan 'Long live the Federation and death to the Unitarist savages'. To top it off, he even revived the slave trade for a while. Eventually his enemies – and they were plenty – united against him. Rosas was overthrown in 1852 and fled the country on a British steamer bound for Southampton, where he blew a fortune trying to recreate an Argentine *estancia* in the heart of the English countryside.

With Rosas out of the way, Argentina was soon well on track to becoming a nation state. A federal constitution was established in 1853. In 1862, Bartolomé Mitre was sworn in as the first president of the Republic and Buenos Aires city's status was formalised by 1886, when it was made a Federal Capital.

Argentina now faced a dilemma. It had an abundance of glorious fertile land and a miserable lack of people. The country was desperate for cultivation and colonisation.

FROM THE BOATS

The response was massive immigration as Argentina turned to Europe for capital and people. Boats landed at the bustling port of Buenos Aires, and out of them poured immigrants in their droves. Between 1857 and 1924 more than 5.5 million people came to Argentina; over 3 million stayed. The majority were from the Mediterranean countries – half were Italians, a quarter were Spaniards. But immigrants also came from Germany, Britain, Russia, Poland, France and the Middle East. Among them were land speculators, entrepreneurs and romantic adventurers, but mostly they were poor Europeans seeking a better life in the New World. Immigration remained a government priority for the better part of a century and has intrinsically shaped present-day Argentina. By 1914, one-third of the country's population had been born abroad and 80 per cent of the country were either immigrants or their children.

'The history of Buenos Aires is written in its telephone directory,' writes Bruce Chatwin in his now legendary *In Patagonia*. A random selection among the 'Rs' throws up a Romanov, a Rommel, a Radziwil, a Rose and a Rothschild. They're all still there today in addition to an even more exotic roll call as Argentina continues to welcome immigrants from across the globe.

Other Latin Americans are fond of reminding their aloof and arrogant neighbour in the south of its humble beginnings. 'The Bolivians and Peruvians come from the Incas,' they boast. 'The Guatemalans come from the Maya and the Mexicans from the Aztecs. But the Argentines,' they sneer, 'they come from the boats.'

'The truth,' say the Argentines, 'is that the rest of Latin America is plain jealous. We're taller, blonder and richer.'

INDIANS

The fact that the Argentines are on the whole taller and fairer than their Latin American neighbours remains a sensitive subject – Argentina's indigenous population was quickly and ruthlessly obliterated. There was practically no chance for the native people to mix with their European counterparts to create a dominant *mestizo* race that is so characteristic of Mexico and other Latin American nations.

Indian communities in pre-Conquest Argentina never reached anywhere near the enormous numbers found in Central America and Peru. Historian David Rock estimates that at the time of the Conquest they numbered no more than between 750,000 and quite possibly half that number. With only two people for every three square miles, many lived as nomadic hunters and gatherers. Tribes such as the Querandí roamed the pampas, where they would hunt rheas (a type of ostrich) and guanacos (a type of llama) with *boleadores* (weighted three-thonged lassos). In the far south, the Yamana Indians speared seals and fish and travelled in canoes. More organised and sedentary groups such as the Diaguita inhabited the north of the country. But north and south, all of them were vulnerable. Those that survived the Spanish Conquest and its aftermath were later slaughtered during the state-sponsored 'desert campaigns' of the 19th century. At one stage during this particularly gruesome chapter of Argentina's history, local landowners offered a gold sovereign for each Indian ear.

Today, remaining indigenous groups form less than 2 per cent of the total population (some estimates are as low as 0.5 per cent), while mestizos (people with mixed European and Indian ancestry) account for less than 15 per cent. Most of these indigenous communities are found in the far north of the country on the Paraguayan, Bolivian and Brazilian borders. The largest groups are the Quechua, Toba, Wichi and Guaraní but there are also isolated groups of Mapuche and Tehuelche Indians still living in Patagonia.

Many live in conditions of extreme poverty on the fringes of Argentine society and fight a constant battle to uphold their cultural identity and rights in a country where the expression *Que Indio* is still used to describe a barbarian and people go out of their way to point out that they are from 'good European stock' and have no 'Indian' blood.

THE PERÓNS

With the coming of the immigrants, Argentina entered an astonishing period of growth and prosperity, to emerge the world's sixth richest nation. In France they even had a saying, *riche comme un Argentin,* thanks to the extravagantly wealthy Argentines who holidayed in Paris. But the country's money remained in the hands of the oligarchy and *estancieros* (large landowners), many of whom lived on *estancias* (ranches) the size of small kingdoms. Few of the immigrants ever made it out of the cities and by the early 20th century an increasingly militant and urban working class began clamouring for social change. It was to these dissatisfied masses that Juan Domingo Perón appealed.

Few names from Argentina's turbulent past still conjure up such emotion as that of Perón, both General Juan Domingo Perón and his charismatic wife Evita. Perón came to prominence on the back of a military coup in 1943 and was soon made head of the labour ministry, where he built up a powerful base among the trade unions and urban working class. He married Evita, his glamorous mistress and an aspiring actress, in a secret ceremony a few months before he was elected president in 1946. He remained president until 1955. Together, the Peróns promised a 'New Argentina' founded on social justice and economic independence. They didn't make much of an attempt to hide their hatred for the upper classes. Evita once declared that 'There are two things of which I am proud: my love for the people and my hatred for the oligarchy.' Not to be outdone by his wife's idealism, Perón had the Jockey Club – the bastion of the upper classes in Buenos Aires – burnt down.

Argentina remains divided on the issue of the Peróns to this day. Perón's supporters – known as *peronistas* – argue that Peron's administration brought about striking social reforms including the introduction of state pensions, workers' rights and full legal status for the trade unions. *Peronista* members of the Justicialist Party (the formal name given to the Peronist political party) still chant Perón's name and march beneath banners of Evita's face. Anti-*peronistas* brand Perón a dictator, drawing attention to his Nazi ties and secret bank accounts, and holding him accountable for the economic ruin of the country.

In 1955, Perón was ousted by yet another military coup. He fled first to Paraguay and later to Spain, where he lived in stately exile for the next 17 years, finally returning to Argentina in 1973.

'Don't cry for me, Argentina'

Depending on whether or not you're a *peronista*, Evita is either a saint or a sinner – there is no middle ground. As the illegitimate child of Juan Duarte and Juana Ibarguren, Evita's beginnings were remarkably humble. She grew up in a small dreary town in the pampas, living with four brothers and sisters in a modest house which her mother ran as a *pensión*. At the tender age of 15, she left for Buenos Aires with a tango singer, hoping to make it as an actress. But for years she barely scraped by. Half-starved, she would act for just a cup of milky coffee. Eventually she made it as a radio actress but her ignominious beginnings and illegitimacy always hung over her.

Even as the president's wife, Evita was consistently snubbed by Argentina's elite. The ultimate affront came when the aristocratic ladies of Buenos Aires society refused to grant her the presidency of the Benevolent Ladies Trust charity, an honour traditionally given to all of Argentina's First Ladies. Not one to take a back seat in life, Evita dyed her hair blonde, dressed up in Dior, shut down the Benevolent Ladies and set up her own charity, the Eva Perón Foundation. Swarms of the poor flocked to the foundation's office in the labour ministry, where Evita directed the construction of hundreds of hospitals, schools and clinics across the country and in moments of abandon handed out 50 and 100 peso notes, bicycles, sewing machines and false teeth to her shirtless ones or *descamisados* as she called them. They called her – and still call her – the Spiritual Chief of the Nation, Lady of Hope, Leader of the Humble and even Saint Evita.

Photo: Archive Photos

Eva Perón – saint or sinner?

When she died of uterine cancer in 1952 at the age of 33, forty thousand Argentines wrote to the Pope to demand her immediate canonisation. Half a million mourners queued for hours to kiss her coffin and some people even tried to commit suicide around her body as it lay in state. The country remained in mourning for weeks.

But Evita's power did not die with her. Her face, whether that of the angry woman clutching a microphone or the young, smiling, airbrushed blonde, is regularly used on *peronista* campaign posters today and appears framed on the walls of *peronista* households throughout the country. Her nuclear-proof tomb in Recoleta cemetery is now one of the country's top tourist attractions.

Evita is still a name that continues to arouse hot emotions across Argentina. So when Alan Parker's film *Evita,* based on Andrew Lloyd Webber and Tim Rice's musical, was released in 1997, it was bound to cause controversy. Once again, a lavishly dressed blonde leant over the balcony of the Casa Rosada, only this time it was the material girl Madonna, belting out the heart-wrenching *Don't cry for me, Argentina*. As you can well guess, this infuriated the country's *peronistas*. Here was Madonna, a racy pop star, not to mention a *yankee*, playing the role of their beloved Evita. The matter wasn't helped by the fact that the script hinted that their spiritual leader had slept her way to the top. The vice-president (a *peronista*) urged people to boycott the film, two cinemas showing *Evita* were smoke-bombed and a professional wrestler challenged Parker to a duel with the director's weapon of choice!

The fact that more than 40 years since her death Evita can still provoke such turmoil speaks for itself. Her legend, like her embalmed body which lies in Recoleta cemetery, is indestructible.

THE DIRTY WAR

Although Perón did not return to Argentina until 1973, throughout his years of exile *peronismo* – the force behind Perón – remained a major feature in Argentina. Governments came and went but none came anywhere near the popularity that Perón had achieved in the 1940s and 1950s. By the early 1970s pro-*peronista* guerrilla groups had started to emerge. They staged regular high-profile kidnappings and bank robberies and the country steadily plunged into chaos and anarchy. Perón's return to Argentina in 1973 seemed like an obvious solution and he was promptly elected president with 60 per cent of the vote. Less than a year into his presidency, Perón died and Argentina was left under the control of his third and largely incompetent wife, Isabelita, a former nightclub dancer whom he had met in Panama. As you can imagine, it didn't take long for the generals to step in again and form a ruling military junta under General Jorge Videla.

What happened next is undoubtedly the blackest chapter of Argentina's recent history and remains an open wound in Argentina's conscience. From 1976 until 1983, Argentina remained under the control of a series of military juntas. During this period, chillingly

Silhouettes of the disappeared in Buenos Aires' Plaza de Mayo.

dubbed *El Proceso* (the Process), the armed forces waged a bloody and indiscriminate 'Dirty War' against thousands of supposed 'subversives'.

The guerrilla groups, which had been active since 1970, were the military's primary targets. These were comprised of mainly young professionals and students, often with affluent middle-class backgrounds. Most were in their 20s and there were large numbers of young female combatants. The military's reprisals were far worse than anything the leftist guerrilla groups had carried out. While the guerrillas may have killed 200–300 people at the most, *El Proceso* claimed the lives of tens of thousands of Argentines. Human rights groups estimate that as many as 30,000 people were killed or 'disappeared' during this time.

No one was above suspicion and thousands of Argentines were taken from their homes, rounded up and sent to clandestine torture centres across the country. Victims included trade unionists, socialists, psychologists, human rights and other activists, nuns, priests, pacifists, journalists, teachers, lawyers, doctors, students, children, pensioners and housewives. They were bundled into Ford Falcons and driven off by men in dark glasses, never to be seen again. (Even today, 20 years later, the sight of a Ford Falcon can send a shiver down many a spine.)

The military government repeatedly denied the existence of the torture centres and of the prisoners held there. With no official status, the prisoners did not exist – they had 'disappeared'. All the prisoners were, without exception, systematically tortured. The torturers were after names and addresses of dissidents allegedly involved in subversive activities. But more often than not, the victims were innocent bystanders caught up in the witch-hunt – they had no names to give.

Inside the torture centres, prisoners were submitted to electric shocks, continual beatings and mock executions. Some were buried up to their necks in the ground and left there for days. Others were forced to witness the torture of their own families. Then finally, when no more could be done with them, they were thrown from planes into the Río de la Plata – many of them drugged and still alive.

Ironically, it was the war against Britain over the Falklands/ Malvinas Islands in 1982 that brought about the end of military rule in Argentina. The military's ignominious defeat by crack British troops and the capture of 10,000 Argentine soldiers further discredited a military government that was also facing economic ruin and increasing pressure from the families of the 'disappeared'. General Leopoldo Galtieri, who headed the military junta at that time, was promptly booted out of the Casa Rosada, and millions of exuberant Argentines greeted the subsequent return to democracy in 1983.

GOVERNMENT STRUCTURE AND KEY POLITICAL ISSUES

With democracy once again restored in Argentina, the government returned to the principles of the 1853 constitution. This was revised in 1994 with 19 new articles, 40 amendments and an additional chapter on New Rights and Guarantees. Argentina has a federal system of government along the lines of the United States. There are three branches of authority: the executive, headed by the president; the judiciary, headed by the Supreme Court of nine judges; and the legislative, which consists of a bicameral national Congress of 257 directly elected congressmen, each serving a four-year term, and 72 senators (three per province, three from the Federal Capital) who will each serve a six-year term as of 2001. The president and vice-president are directly elected for a four-year term renewable once.

Argentina has more than 20 political parties, among them the centre-left Frente del Pais Solidario (Frepaso) and the more moderate Unión Cívica Radical (UCR). They united to form the victorious Alliance in the 1999 election under Fernando De la Rua. The *peronistas* (Justicialist Party) are still a massive and active political force in the country. They were in power between 1989 and 1999 under President Carlos Saul Menem.

As the first democratically elected president since the return to civilian rule in 1983, President Raúl Alfonsín from the Radical Party was faced with the delicate task of dealing with the military. He put former junta members on trial and several high-ranking military officials were jailed for crimes against humanity committed during the Dirty War. But under increasing pressure and a threatened military uprising in 1987, Alfonsín was eventually forced to concede to the military. He passed two controversial laws which absolved lower-ranking military officers from crimes on the grounds that they were simply acting under orders and put a moratorium on all trials. When President Carlos Menem won the 1989 election, he surprised the nation further when he pardoned and released General Jorge Videla and other military officers from jail – Menem himself had been imprisoned under the military junta. However, the military's role has been considerably weakened, the defence budget has been cut and the armed forces have been purged of anti-democratic officers.

Ownership of the Falkland Islands, known as Las Islas Malvinas in Argentina, continues to be a bone of contention (see Chapter 7), with successive governments pledging their return to Argentina. But the biggest challenge faced by the new democracy was getting the shambolic economy back on to a stronger footing.

THE ECONOMIC SITUATION

Argentina is fabulously rich in natural resources and has a highly educated, skilled population of 36 million. As much as 88 per cent of the country is urban and a third of the population live in greater Buenos Aires, making this the economic as well as the political hub of the country. Fanning out from Buenos Aires is the pampas – expansive fertile grasslands that are justly famous for producing top-quality wheat and cattle. Sugar and tobacco thrive in the north, and the south is home to vast sheep stations and rich supplies of largely untapped minerals. Argentina is also self-sufficient in petroleum and other energy resources.

Agriculture and agro-industry remain of major importance in Argentina's economy. Agro-industry alone accounts for 30 per cent of the nation's GDP and 63 per cent of export earnings. However, manufacturing of iron, steel, cars, textiles, industrial chemicals, machinery, transport equipment and hydroelectric power is also important. The country's trade unions remain well developed and independent, although they do not hold the massive political clout they once did under Perón.

All this seems like the perfect scenario for a booming economy, and indeed Argentina is one of Latin America's wealthiest countries. Yet years of political chaos, military intervention and ineffectual civilian rule has meant that Argentina's economy has never managed to fulfil its vast potential. A leading question that still confounds observers is 'what went wrong?' Why was one of the richest countries in the world in 1914, exporting half the world's beef and much of its wheat and grain supplies, by the 1980s burdened by unemployment, poverty and a crippling foreign debt (reaching an astronomical all-time high of US$65 billion in 1990). Argentina is also the only country in the world to have suffered more than 15 years of continuous triple-digit inflation. By 1989, inflation had reached an annual level of over 4,000 per cent!

Initial attempts by President Alfonsín to curb inflation failed when he introduced a new currency in 1985 under the Austral Plan. But it was President Menem who came up with the biggest surprise. Once elected in 1989, he introduced a free-market system and austere monetary measures. He tightened the law to reduce tax evasion and stabilised spiralling inflation with the convertibility law which pegged the new Argentine peso to the US dollar. Menem also launched an intensive privatisation programme. Argentina's telephone company, airlines, most railways, electric power generation companies, national oil company, steel mills, ports, airports, TV stations and most public services have been transferred to the private sector.

The downside to this programme, however, has been massive

Photo: Jamie Grant

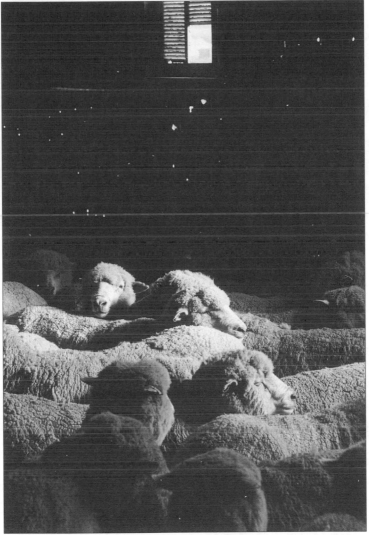

Sheep farming is an important part of Argentina's economy.

31

layoffs and rising unemployment. The economy was also hit hard by the 'Tequila crisis' in 1995 (following Mexico's economic collapse) and has suffered from the recent devaluation of the Brazilian real (30 per cent of Argentina's exports go to Brazil). Much remains to be done to extend the recent economic gains, dismantle old barriers to growth and bring down the rate of unemployment.

Still, the government has resisted pressures to devalue the currency, inflation remains at its lowest level in 20 years and Argentina looks set on a path of stable, sustainable growth.

NATIONAL EMBLEMS

Argentina's national flag has three horizontal stripes of light blue, white and light blue. In the middle of the white stripe is a brilliant golden sun. The national flower is the ceibo and the national stone is the manganese spar or the 'rose of the Inca'.

Chapter Two

THE COUNTRY

'All grass and sky, and sky and grass, and still more sky and grass.'

—R.B. Cunningham Graham, on
Argentina's famously flat pampas

Argentina is an immense and stunning land that incorporates every possible type of climate, altitude and landscape you can imagine – and a lot more that defies imagination until you've seen it with your own eyes. The simple truth is, wherever you decide to settle in Argentina, you'll be ridiculously spoilt for choice.

Argentina is the eighth largest country in the world – the second largest in South America after Brazil – and only marginally smaller than India. For administrative purposes it is divided into 23 provinces and the city of Buenos Aires, which is classified as a federal district. The physical characteristics vary tremendously between the provinces and even within each province. The country's main geographic features, however, range from the dense subtropical forests of the north to the Andes mountains in the west and the vast grassy plains of the pampas that fan out from Buenos Aires down into the Patagonian plateaux of the south. *'Gracias a la vida'* – 'Thank you life,' sings Mercedes Sosa, Argentina's much-loved folk singer, in her deep, rich voice. 'You've given me so much; cities and lakes, beaches and deserts, mountains and plains.' You can see her point exactly.

As if this geographical mosaic isn't enough, Argentina also lays claim to the Falkland Islands, known locally as Las Islas Malvinas, as well as the more obscure Shag and Black Rocks, South Georgia, the South Sandwich Islands, the South Shetland Islands, the South Orkney Islands and a considerable slice of Antarctica. Although such territorial claims are internationally disputed, it's illegal to print a map in Argentina stating anything otherwise.

As proof of this enormous geographical diversity, Argentines don't even have to leave their own country to travel to new horizons. During the summer vacations over January and February, they flock to the seaside towns on the Atlantic coast, briefly swelling the ranks of these small coastal cities to millions. Others venture further afield into the windswept plains of Patagonia, as far south as Tierra del Fuego, or up into the scrubby northwest. If they do get the itch to go abroad, they just make the short trip across the chocolate brown waters of the Río de la Plata to reach neighbouring Uruguay, where the chicest and richest Argentines own luxurious summer houses.

Despite the fact that Argentines are said to hanker after all things European and North American, they are incredibly proud of their own country and will profess to know everything about each place even if they haven't been there themselves. If you enjoy solitude and crowd-free places don't take their travel advice too seriously. Argentines are social creatures by habit and love to go where the action (and everybody else) is. Moreover, *porteños*, who secretly believe that Buenos Aires is the only place to live, will be horrified if you mention that you might go to Patagonia out of season or, when it comes down to it, choose to live anywhere outside the confines of *Capital Federal*.

It won't take you long to discover that there are two Argentinas: Buenos Aires and the rest of the country simply referred to as 'the Interior'. According to the inflexible law of Argentine geography, if you're not in Buenos Aires city, you will be in the Interior. For visitor and native alike, they are worlds apart. A sheep farmer from Santa Cruz province in Argentina's deep south will be just as disoriented in Buenos Aires as a sophisticated *porteño* suddenly finding himself on a Patagonian *estancia*. The beauty of this setup, however, is that you can skip between cosmopolitan chic and the infinite diversity of the countryside – it's just a plane, train or bus ride away.

BUENOS AIRES

Given this tantalising choice, it seems surprising that more than a third of the country's population have chosen to live in Buenos Aires or its suburbs. Argentina's capital is a powerful magnet that continuously draws Argentines from the provinces and other Latin Americans from neighbouring countries. It is the country's political, economic and social hub, and most of the people who live there wouldn't have it any other way. (A plan in 1986 to move the capital to the Patagonian city of Viedma was greeted with such screams of horror by the *porteños* that it had to be smartly dropped.) 'If God were an Argentine,' goes a local *porteño* saying, 'then he would live in Buenos Aires.'

The downside of this human condensation is smouldering pollution (rapidly on its way to rival that of Mexico City and Brazil's São Paulo) and unrelenting noise levels that defy all human experience. Pollution and noise, however, will soon be forgiven as you enjoy being in one of the world's most sophisticated cities, one that justly deserves its nickname, 'the Paris of South America'.

All cities have their own tempo, but the difference is that Buenos Aires' races at about 100 miles per hour. It is a huge, pumping, vibrating, living and breathing metropolis, the proverbial city that never sleeps. And if you like to party, it is heaven. The natives of Buenos Aires, the *porteños* (people of the port), have an almost religious fanaticism about their beloved city. 'To me it is a fairy tale that Buenos Aires was founded,' wrote Jorge Luis Borges, one of the most famous *porteños*. 'It seems as eternal as water and air.'

The first thing you must get to grips with, should you choose Buenos Aires for your home, is that *porteños* defy all sensible laws of sleep. They appear to survive on a diet of endless coffee and catnaps, interspersed with a frenzied social life. Maybe it's thanks to a Latin temperament or the fact that they can't bear to miss out on a social gathering – in Buenos Aires there's always something going on somewhere – that *porteños* are up all hours of the day and night.

Buenos Aires really comes awake at night. Restaurants, cafés and fabulously stacked bookstalls don't close up just because the sun's gone down. Then of course there are the discos, some with capacity for several thousand, where sleek and glamorous *porteños* congregate for hours of endless partying. And don't miss out on the tango bars where couples cling to each other passionately into the small hours of the morning. For the novice, and even for *porteños* themselves, this pace of life is exhausting. 'Buenos Aires kills you,' *porteño* friends tell me. 'But there's no way we would dream of living anywhere else.'

THE INTERIOR

Argentina's Interior has a thoroughly South American feel to it, and just a few hours' drive from downtown Buenos Aires you'll be mingling with modern-day gauchos and enormous herds of horned cattle and enjoying magnificent unpolluted sunsets. There's even time for that great stress buster, the siesta.

Generally, the further south you travel from Buenos Aires, the colder and more desolate it gets, until you arrive in Tierra del Fuego and its capital Ushuaia, which makes the bold – and cold – claim to be the southernmost city in the world. Apart from a cluster of sparsely populated and unforgiving islands, you can go no further south (unless a trip to Antarctica is on your itinerary).

Heading north from Buenos Aires, you start to shed your clothes as a blissful subtropical climate kicks in and lush grassy plains give way to thick forests and vast muddy rivers filled with toucans and caimans (the crocodile's South American cousin). Westward, the Andes mountain chain swells to awesome peaks, creating an almost impenetrable barrier between Argentina and Chile. Eastward lie the Atlantic Ocean and 5,000 km of coastline and windswept beaches.

These are Argentina's natural boundaries, yet you're hardly likely to feel penned in or wanting to leave. Driving the 3,500 km from the Bolivian border in the north to Ushuaia in the far south could take you weeks. You'll be lucky if you can make the time.

For ease, Argentina's mainland territory of 2.8 million square kilometres can be divided into four major geographic regions: the central pampas, the Andes to the west, the fertile lowland north and Patagonia in the south.

The Pampas

This vast sweeping grassland plain fans out westward from Buenos Aires, running for more than a thousand miles from the Atlantic Ocean to the foothills of the Andes and stretching from the Gran Chaco region in the north to the Río Colorado in the south.

For many, Argentina *is* the pampas. Flat as a billiard table, this is ideal terrain for crops and livestock. Cattle are clearly in heaven here, grazing upon acres of lush grasses – no wonder they so generously provide us with such succulent steaks. The flat horizon of the pampas is broken only by the buildings of an occasional *estancia* surrounded by weeping willows, eucalyptus groves, stately poplars and twisted ombú trees – emerging like islands in a sea of grass and sky. Geographically, its flatness may seem uninteresting, yet the pampas has its own magic – sunsets and sunrises that will knock your socks off and a mean wind that periodically whips itself up into the terrifyingly boisterous *pampero*.

The Andes

Forming the backbone of South America, the Andes runs down the entire length of Argentina along its border with Chile, reaching some of its highest peaks. It is in the province of San Juan that the awesome Mount Aconcagua rises to a breathtaking 6,960 meters. In the northern provinces of Salta, La Rioja, San Juan and Mendoza, the foothills of the Andes are filled with vineyards. In the southern province of Neuquén and the western parts of Río Negro, Chubut and Santa Cruz, they become glacial lakes and giant ice fields.

This is the side of Argentina you want to get near if you enjoy adventure sports – skiing, climbing, white-water rafting or just straightforward walking. Hugging the Andes from north to south is the famous Route 40, which crosses through scrubby deserts of fat-fingered cacti and the Lake District into Patagonia. With only a third asphalted, Route 40 is the ideal adventure for off-roaders.

The North

In the north of the country, heading eastward from the Andes, the dry mountainous landscape of Salta and Jujuy gives way to the hot scrubby plains of the Gran Chaco – an enormous area that stretches into Paraguay and parts of Brazil and Bolivia. The Chaco engulfs the two Argentine provinces of Chaco and Formosa. Much of this region is completely inaccessible and the western part of Chaco province, a vast uninhabited area, is dubbed *El Impenetrable*.

Further east still, you cross the Paraná River and enter the provinces of Entre Ríos, Corrientes and Misiones, an area known as Mesopotamia. Bordered on one side by the Paraná and on the other

White-water rafting in San Juan.

by the River Uruguay, the area has traditionally felt cut off from the rest of the country, but the fertile terrain has made it an important livestock and agricultural centre and great fishing country.

Misiones, the northeasternmost point of Argentina, rises like an isthmus squeezed between Paraguay and Brazil. Here you have the spectacular Iguazú falls, set in 55,000 hectares of national parkland and subtropical forests. The falls can be viewed from both the Argentine and Brazilian sides, but as the local saying goes, 'The Brazilian side may have the best views but we put on the show.' If it looks familiar, that's because it played the grisly backdrop to the opening scenes of Roland Joffe's 1986 epic film *The Mission*. The area had been the centre of Jesuit activity, where the local Guaraní Indians were placed in *reducciónes* (specially designed communities). Many of the ruins are still visible today.

Patagonia

If any name has the ability to bewitch, surely it must be that of Patagonia. This strange land begins at the Colorado River at 39°S and rolls on down through pastoral steppe and glacial fields to the Magellan Straits at the southernmost tip of the continent. It is sparsely populated, practically treeless and internationally famous for its wind. 'Patagonia without wind,' goes a local saying, 'would be like hell without the devil.'

Early explorers claimed that Patagonia was inhabited by naked giants and monsters. In fact, its name is believed to have come from the explorer Magellan, who allegedly crossed paths with a giant there, looked down at his feet and declared, 'Ha, Patagon!' – Wow, big feet! is a close-enough translation. Latter-day travel writer Bruce Chatwin remembers Patagonia from his school days as the safest place to be in the event of a nuclear attack. And lately it has also been getting a reputation for dinosaurs, which are being unearthed at an alarming rate from Patagonia's arid plains. Discoveries include the 8-ton predator Giganotosaurus, which makes T. Rex look like his little brother in comparison, and the 100-ton plant-eating Argentinosaurus – the biggest herbivore discovered to date.

Photo: Jamie Grant

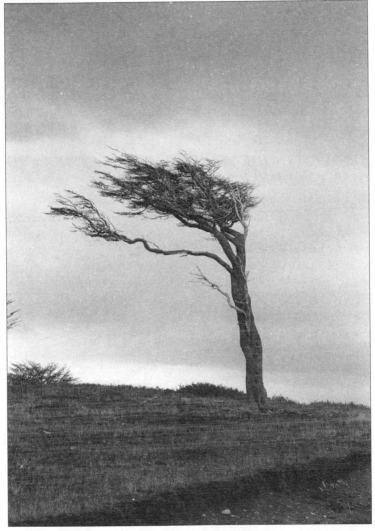

Windswept and barren, the Patagonian landscape is broken up by the occasional tree, twisted by relentless wind.

Patagonia has also harboured many an outlaw in its past, including the famous North American bandit duo, Butch Cassidy and the Sundance Kid, but today Patagonia also belongs to the rich and famous of the world. *Estancia* owners are purported to include Jane Fonda, CNN's Ted Turner, billionaire businessman George Soros, Italian fashion magnate Luciano Benetton, restaurateur Charlie Lewis and actor Christopher Lambert, all of whom rub shoulders with the locals and an awful lot of sheep.

A ROUGH GUIDE TO ARGENTINA'S CITIES AND OUTSTANDING FEATURES

Yes, there is life outside Buenos Aires, even if the *porteño* tries to tell you otherwise. The following key cities and features are listed in order of their distance by road from Buenos Aires city. So you can judge just how far away – or how close – you want to get from the heaving metropolis. Population indicators are given: ***million plus, **half million plus, *100,000 plus; no asterisk means it is a smaller city.

La Plata**

(64 km southeast of BA)
The capital of Buenos Aires province, La Plata is renowned for its spectacular natural history museum, university and lots of grandiose public buildings. Designed with Washington, DC in mind, the city was built practically from scratch in 1882. There are no street names, only numbers.

Luján

(65 km west of BA)
Dubbed the 'Holy City', Luján welcomes 4 million pilgrims a year, who come to pay homage to Argentina's patron saint, the Virgin of Luján. A statue of the Virgin is kept in Luján's neo-Gothic basilica, whose twin towers rise above the small town in a lovely riverside setting.

Rosario***

(295 km northeast of BA)

Affectionately nicknamed the Chicago of Argentina, Rosario is the third largest city in the country, thanks to its strategic location and bustling port on the Río Paraná. Che Guevara was born here as well as many of Argentina's great rock musicians. You'll soon have to choose which side to support in the ferocious football scene between Newells Old Boys and Rosario Central.

Mar del Plata**

(418 km southeast of BA)

More of a beach town than a city, Mar del Plata is the centre for the sea fishing industry. It also claims the biggest casino in the world (come dressed to kill). In the summer months of January and February the city's ranks swell from 500 thousand to 3 million with the massive migration of sun-seeking *porteños*. If you can find any room on the beach, this is the place to be seen in summer. (Although the serious money swans off to Punta del Este in Uruguay.)

Paraná

(507 km north of BA)

The capital of Entre Ríos province is close to large forestry, citrus plantations and cattle ranches. It sits on the eastern bank of the Río Paraná, just 27 km from the city of Santa Fé. The two cities are connected by the Hernandarias tunnel, which runs beneath the river.

Bahia Blanca*

(637 km southwest of BA)

An industrial centre and well-run port with a natural harbour, the city was originally built as a fort against marauding Indians. Agriculture and petrochemicals are the mainstay of this city, which is set to become a major terminal for exports of liquid petroleum. It is also an important naval base.

Córdoba***

(701 km northwest of BA)

Argentina's attractive second largest city is an important industrial centre with a strong history of militancy. The people are warm and friendly, speak in singsong accents and are slightly more down to earth than in Buenos Aires. Córdoba has wonderful colonial buildings, including a magnificent cathedral that dates from the 17th century. It swarms with young medics studying at Argentina's oldest university. It is also the gateway to the sierras of Córdoba, rolling hills and lakes that bring to mind the Swiss Alps in summer.

Corrientes* and Resistencia*

(936 km and 1,008 km north of BA)

These sister cities lie on opposite banks of the fast-flowing Río Paraná. Resistencia, the capital of Chaco province, is the quieter of the two. Graham Greene chose Corrientes province with its appropriate backdrop of red earth and tropical palm trees as the setting for a kidnapping in *The Honorary Consul*. This area is the hub of northeast Argentina's agricultural industry. There's great carnival and great fishing. Keep an eye out for the aggressive dorado and the enormous surubi catfish, which can weigh as much as a large man – or better still, catch one yourself in the *corrientino's* classic weekend getaway at Paso de la Patria.

Mendoza**

(1,044 km west of BA)

The wine capital of Argentina, Mendoza is surrounded by vineyards at the foot of the Andes. Huge plazas and wide, sweeping avenues make this one of the loveliest cities in Argentina, which can also boast 350 days of sunshine a year. It has a big-city feel and is modern and well laid out, but life seems slower here. Don't miss the wine festival held in the first week of March.

San Juan*

(1,106 km northwest of BA)

Old-fashioned sun worshippers will simply adore San Juan which averages 9 hours of sun a day and only 100 mm of rainfall a year. Unfortunately it was also built on a fault line and most of the city was flattened by a massive earthquake in 1944. San Juan is now blessed with relatively few skyscrapers and beautiful tree-lined avenues. It is surrounded by vineyards and has a complicated but breathtaking system of dams.

La Rioja*

(1,159 km northwest of BA)

Founded in 1591, much of La Rioja's colonial architecture survived an earthquake in 1894. La Rioja is small, quiet and provincial with the Sierra de Velasco hills as a backdrop It is known as the city of orange trees and is also a big wine producer. There are hot springs, canyons and dramatic rock formations nearby.

Tucumán**

(1,202 km northwest of BA)

San Miguel de Tucumán (its full name) is the city where history was made in 1816 when independence from Spain was formally declared. Glimpses of its former grandeur are seen in a massive park filled with monuments and statues of the heroes of independence and a beautiful colonial plaza in the centre. It is otherwise slightly shabby but friendly. Nearby are the Indian ruins of the fortified city at Quilmes, well worth a visit, although it is unbearably hot in summer.

The Iguazú Falls

(1,285 km north of BA)

When Eleanor Roosevelt laid eyes on the Iguazú falls rumour has it that she just shook her head and said, 'Poor Niagara!' You can walk a few inches above the falls on a hair-raising system of catwalks. Don't look down at their corroded concrete foundations but keep your eyes open for the fabulous butterflies and bird life, including toucans, in this dramatic jungle setting. Terrifying boat trips take you up to the falls themselves, where no less than 5,000 cubic meters of water per second plunge over a 70 metre drop.

Península Valdés

(1,291 km south of BA)
There is a national park here, near the port city of Puerto Madryn on the windswept Atlantic coast. Take a boat trip to see whales, orcas, sealions, elephant seals and penguins. In summer, Puerto Madryn fills up with Argentines who come for the beaches, wildlife and good scuba diving. In winter the area takes on a deserted air and even the penguins leave.

Gaimán

(1,340 km southwest of BA)
Famous for its Welsh immigrants who arrived in 1865, Gaimán is probably the best-known Welsh village in the region, largely thanks to its splendid teahouses. Much of the local population still have Welsh names like Jones and Edwards and even speak a little Welsh. Gaimán even holds an annual eisteddfod. Welsh chapels and delightful cottages overgrown with roses make this a green and pleasant, if not a little peculiar, oasis in the flat Patagonian landscape.

Cafayate

(1,380 km northwest of BA)
This classic whitewashed *pueblo* is enchanting and it's easy to understand why it is so popular with tourists from all across Argentina. The whole town is hemmed in by rows and rows of vineyards. The Calchaquie valleys are nearby with small attractive colonial towns such as Cachi and Molinos.

Salta*

(1,508 km northwest of BA)

This colonial city with a beautiful plaza surrounded by outdoor cafés, whitewashed balustraded buildings and springlike temperatures all year round is a popular holiday destination. You get spectacular views from the San Bernardo mountain accessible by stone stairs or cable car. Salta is also home to the *empanada* – these cheese or meat patties are sold on every street corner. There are also good gaucho festivals.

Jujuy*

(1,536 km northwest of BA)

Pronounced 'Hoo Hooey', the city's full name is San Salvador de Jujuy and it is the capital of one of Argentina's poorest and more isolated provinces. Relics of former colonial glory compete with dilapidated ruins, post-earthquake architecture and divine orange trees. A chaotic black market opposite the bus station peddles everything from coca leaves to flip-flops. Nearby is the Humahuaca valley with its spectacular arid landscapes and famous folkloric festivals.

Bariloche

(1,597 km southwest of BA)

Bariloche is reminiscent of a Swiss ski resort with its chocolate-box scenery of woods and mountains on the shore of the 96 km long Lake Nahuel Huapí. It enjoys fierce rivalry with Las Leñas for skiing, but Bariloche wins hands-down for its buzzing social life. The town itself has a year-round holiday atmosphere and is packed with clubs and discos that charge a small fortune at the door.

Comodoro Rivadavia*

(1,711 km south of BA)

The centre of Argentina's petroleum industry, Comodoro Rivadavia is the largest city in Patagonia's Chubut province. It is a modern coastal town (no plazas here) whose rise has been tied to the oil industry. To the south are beach resorts where you can observe sealions – the water may be too icy for a swim yourself. Further afield are the Cuevas de las Manos, prehistoric caves with 10,000-year-old images of hands, guanacos and other animals stencilled on the walls.

Río Gallegos
(2,484 km south of BA)
There isn't much to see in the city itself, but as the capital of Santa Cruz province, it is strategically placed at the end of the world, a human oasis in a land of sweeping Patagonian plains, enormous skies and rough seas, where sheep outnumber men 50 to one.

El Calafate
(2,732 km southwest of BA)
El Calafate is criticised in guidebooks for being touristy with inflated prices, but its location on the southern shore of Lake Argentino is so beautiful that many *porteños* have decided to up sticks and live there permanently (and make a killing off the gringos). The town's population doubles during the summer months as El Calafate is the last port of call for all those going to Los Glaciares National Park.

Los Glaciares National Park
Argentina's second largest national park (600,000 hectares) borders Chile and is home to the Fitzroy mountain range and the famous advancing Moreno glacier, where the occasional tourist used to be killed every season by flying ice. This is the world's third largest ice field (after Antarctica and Greenland) and the lakes and rivers fed by the glaciers have the amazing colours of mineral-rich waters. Scenery freaks will be in heaven. Not to be missed!

Photo: Jamie Grant

Stunning Ushuaia in Tierra del Fuego, the southernmost city in the world.

Ushuaia

(3,070 km south of BA)

Set in a stunning location on the shores of the Beagle Channel in Tierra del Fuego and surrounded by the snowcapped Martial Mountains, Ushuaia captivates. Maybe it's the way the weather constantly changes from snowy blizzards to bright winter sunshine, but the world's southernmost city is also a tax haven and filled with ski centres, a buzzing nightlife and cute huskies from Antarctica. And if you don't like the weather, say the locals, just wait five minutes.

Chapter Three

THE PEOPLE

MELTING POT

'What exists here is a ludicrous form of nationalism. Our entire country is imported. Everybody here is really from somewhere else.'

—Jorge Luis Borges

AN IDENTITY PROBLEM?

How do you begin to describe the Argentines? They are not your Latin American stereotypes, that's for sure. And neither are they really Europeans like their forebears. The Argentine is something of an enigma.

A wit once defined the Argentines as a nation of Italians who speak Spanish, dress as though they're French and like to think they're British. If only it were that simple. Certainly there are millions of descendants of Italians and Spaniards in Argentina. But some in Patagonia speak Welsh and celebrate the eisteddfod. Residents of a village in the mountains of Córdoba don *lederhosen* every October for a German beerfest. Buenos Aires can boast the largest Jewish community outside of Israel (after New York). Sheep farmers in Patagonia still trace their names and sparkling blue eyes back to England, Ireland and Scotland. There are considerable numbers of immigrants from the Middle East, Japan and Asia. The list could go on indefinitely.

The happy result is an exotic mix of customs and cultures, a rainbow of eye colours and a huge variety of accents and mannerisms here in the heart of South America. Everyone knows where they originally came from and will be eager to tell you about their antecedents. Yet at the same time they are all fiercely proud to be Argentines.

Critics are prone to argue that this cultural melting pot means many Argentines are painfully insecure. At times, Argentines themselves complain bitterly that they suffer a complete lack of national identity. An identity crisis would be understandable. They may live in South America's second largest territory, but there is scarcely a trace of native Indian blood among them. Less than 2 per cent of the population can call themselves indigenous, while the vast majority originally came from Europe, thousands of miles away and in another hemisphere. Add to that a penchant for bottled blonde, one of the world's highest rates of plastic surgery and an addiction to psycho-analysis, and no wonder they appear to be walking contradictions!

But are the Argentines really that elusive? Many would disagree. Once you have met them, they are an easily identifiable race, not least by their distinctive accents, notorious good looks, compulsive *mate* drinking and charming if at times infuriating arrogance. 'Abroad, you can recognise an Argentine family a mile off,' says the contemporary Argentine writer Tomás Eloy Martínez. 'Dad in his brown moccasins, the mother's flaming blonde hair ... the gesticulations, everything betrays us.'

SERIOUS ATTITUDE

A popular South American joke, one told enthusiastically by the Argentines themselves, asks, 'What's the best bargain in the world?' The answer: 'Buy an Argentine for what he's worth and sell him for what he thinks he's worth.' Arrogance and a generous dosage of vanity – among both men and women – is an accepted fact of life in Argentina. And why not? They are frequently voted the world's best-looking citizens and I've known men to practically fall over backwards after getting an eyeful of the women in Buenos Aires. No one bats an eyelid if you stop and comb your hair in a reflective surface on the street or casually admire your reflection in a spoon in a restaurant. Nearly all elevators have mirrors, hairdressers and beauty parlours do a roaring trade and at times the whiff of aftershave in nightclubs is quite overpowering. Appearance is everything and it's a rare sight to come across an untidy or unkempt Argentine.

Along with this impossible style and good looks, the Argentine possesses a formidable attitude. No smoking signs, if put up in the first place, are religiously ignored and queues were made to be jumped. Although far from rude, Argentines are not known for their reserved character and won't hesitate to express their opinions, be they political or otherwise. (For this reason, Argentines are occasionally dubbed 'argy-bargies' by unsuspecting foreigners.) I once observed an elegantly dressed man gaily gouging out the eyes of smiling politicians from *peronist* political campaign posters on the street as if it was the most natural thing in the world.

'When you walk into a room you can feel the energy of the Argentines,' an exasperated Uruguayan woman living in Buenos Aires once told me. 'They think that they are number one, that there's nothing or no one above them except God.'

This inflated opinion of themselves gives rise to countless other jibes against Argentines, usually recounted with great relish by other Latin Americans. 'How does an Argentine commit suicide? He throws himself off his own ego!' And have you heard the one about the psychiatrist who asks his colleague to come over immediately as he has an Argentine on his couch with the strangest affliction. 'So?' says his colleague, 'you see lots of Argentines.' 'Yes,' says the psychiatrist, 'but this one's got an inferiority complex!'

The following anecdote may put it better. A German acquaintance was on an Aerolineas Argentinas flight from Buenos Aires to Santiago de Chile. The aeroplane had landed and come to a standstill at the airport but the doors remained firmly locked. After a few minutes of confusion she was horrified to hear the pilot announce over the tannoy that no one would be allowed to disembark until all of the airline's blankets had been returned to the cabin crew. The passengers, mostly Argentines, eventually stood up and casually pulled out the offending articles from their hand luggage which had been neatly tucked away in the overhead lockers. They weren't embarrassed in the least at being caught red-handed pilfering airline property. The

German, new to South America, was momentarily astounded. Later, she found out that she had just witnessed *viveza criolla* – an infamous Argentine attribute – in mass action.

Viveza Criolla and the Vivos

Viveza criolla has been described as anything from 'native cunning' to 'artful lying'. It is a peculiar trait that is both admired and despised, yet it is always carried out in such a charming manner that you simply have to forgive the perpetrator. The man or woman with *viveza criolla* is utterly on the ball, unbelievably quick off the mark in any given situation and always comes out on top. They are known as *vivos*. A good definition of a *vivo* would be that of a man who goes into a revolving door after you but comes out first.

All Argentines, but especially *porteños* (natives of Buenos Aires), are *vivos* to some extent. The most famous Argentine *vivo* that springs to mind is the footballer Diego Maradona, who rose to the top with the help of both wit and skills. His own brand of *viveza criolla* allowed him to score a winning goal with his hand – or the 'hand of God', as he was quick to point out in a post-match interview – and go on to clinch the 1986 World Cup in Mexico. Unlike the passengers on that Aerolineas Argentinas flight, he got away with cheating, and as far as *viveza criolla* is concerned, it's the getting away with it that matters.

Having said this, you don't need to go around worrying that you will be constantly ripped off in Argentina. The majority of Argentines are very honest and have an enormous amount of respect for each other and visitors to the country. People will go out of their way to be helpful and spontaneous acts of generosity – known as *gauchadas* – may surprise you. For every act of *viveza criolla* there will always be a *gauchada* to counteract it.

MACHISMO

In Latin America there's no getting away from machismo – even in this most European of Latin nations. This fierce and often self-destructive mixture of pride and toughness can be seen in everything from the way the men walk – swaggering and proud – to never showing fear, never losing face and never giving in. But Argentine machismo is probably less marked than the Mexican variety. Argentine men, according to my *porteño* friends, are charming and courteous, even if they can be sexist at times. 'It's nice for a change to have doors opened for you,' is the general consensus among female foreigners in Argentina. (In Argentina a man will probably also stand back and allow a woman to step out of the elevator first, give up his seat for a pregnant or elderly woman, buy dinner for his date, walk nearer the street on a pavement to protect his female companion from traffic and pay for her bus ticket.)

Photo: Jamie Grant

It's a man's world ... or is it?

Argentine men make charming if not modest Romeos, and eyeing up girls is a national pastime. It is considered a matter of macho honour to murmur comments at passing women on the street. Such comments, known as *piropos*, are an accepted fact of life and are usually politely ignored. Some men come up with rather eloquent compliments such as 'What's going on in Heaven that the angels have come down to Earth?' They may infuriate feminists but are so much part of Argentine society that I have known women to feel offended when they walk one block without anyone making a comment.

Machismo, however, may be expressed in rather less attractive ways to the fairer sex. Comments on women drivers can be maddening. Once, while boarding a bus whose driver was a woman (practically unheard of), I overheard a man boarding before me saying, 'Good God! How dangerous.' His companion chipped in, 'Why aren't you at home with the kids, darling?'

But hold on a minute. The Argentine male may be turning into a 'New Man'. Recent surveys have shown that more than ever he now goes to the supermarket, looks after the kids and helps out with housework.

GAUCHOS

Someone who wouldn't dream of going to the supermarket is the gaucho, Argentina's answer to the rough, tough American cowboy and the ultimate Argentine *macho*.

The gaucho, and the romance that surrounds him, is one of the strongest symbols of *argentinidad* – Argentina's precarious national identity. He is considered nothing less than a national hero and his antics both on and off his beloved horse are much admired throughout the country. Sadly, the original gaucho is no more. Sheep farming and the introduction of barbed wire along with the concept of private property at the end of the 19th century put an end to his free-riding existence on the open pampas, where he would ride for days in any direction and kill a cow whenever he was hungry.

Yet the legacy of the gaucho is still felt today – not least in the superb horsemanship that practically every Argentine who grows up in the countryside seems to be born with. Many insist that the gaucho is still very much alive and well, just in a more modern mould.

Who was this man that Argentines hold in such high esteem? By all accounts the gaucho was a bloodthirsty, fearless and thoroughly anarchistic individual who answered to no one and would only resort to paid work to keep himself in supplies of rum, tobacco and *yerba mate* – a mildly narcotic tea which helps suppress the appetite and on which he was hooked. It was a lifestyle rather than genes that defined the gaucho. He could be an Indian, a runaway slave, a mestizo or a European. As the 20th century writer Adolfo Bioy Casares pointed out, one of the 'gauchos most gaucho' he had known was a French immigrant called Cipriano Cross.

The gaucho's possessions were few; he owned not much more than his poncho, saddle and horse. His favoured weapon was the *facón,* a lethally sharp curved knife, which he stuck down the back of his *bombachas* (baggy trousers). He would be equally swift to whip out his *facón* to slit his enemy's throat or to cut off a slice of beef and dextrously pop it into his mouth – one slip would mean no tongue!

The wide open pampas was the gaucho's playground where Argentina's famous cattle herds provided an endless source of food. Here he would hunt on horseback, fearlessly whirling *boleadores* to immobilise his prey, which could be anything from small birds and ostriches to fully grown cattle. Nothing phased him except perhaps losing his horse – the real love of his life. This short *gauchesco* verse puts it more succinctly:

My wife and my horse
have gone to Salta.
My wife can stay
but I miss my horse.

Photo: Jamie Grant

A modern-day gaucho rounds up cattle on an estancia *in Misiones.*

A gaucho without a horse was like a man without legs. The horse not only shaped his lifestyle but changed him physically as well. Off his horse, the gaucho was transformed into a lumbering, bow-legged, stooped being. Everything feasible was done on horseback – to be given unmounted work was considered an insult. There are even eyewitness accounts of a gaucho corpse so moulded to the saddle on his horse that he rode to his own funeral!

'His qualities, real and imagined, represent an essential ingredient in the continuous quest by Argentines to define the essence of their national character,' writes Richard W. Slatta, author of the gaucho classic, *Gauchos and the Vanishing Frontier*.

The Modern-day Gaucho

Once you get out into the countryside or visit an *estancia* you will invariably come across men who to all intents and purposes look and behave exactly like these gauchos of old. As you watch them galloping across the plains, effortlessly breaking in horses, lassoing cattle and leaping on and off their mounts, it is obvious that these skills have been passed down from generations of experience. After work they may settle down to drink *mate* and later tuck into huge slabs of meat that have been slowly roasted over an open fire, or slip off to the local *pulpería* (a general store that doubles up as a tavern) to drink, indulge in a little gambling and sing along to the guitar. Many continue to wear the trademark baggy *bombacha* trousers tucked into calfskin boots with a red scarf tied around their neck and a *rastra* (a heavy leather belt decorated with silver coins) around their waist. If you look closely you'll probably be able to spot a *facón* tucked down their waistband. These men may be referred to as *peónes* or ranch hands, but more often than not they are simply called gauchos.

DRIVERS

In the city, the horse has been replaced by the motorcar. Driving is insane and there is much scope for expressing machismo on the roads. 'The Argentine driver is a dangerous driver,' complained a member of the Argentine Automobile Club. 'Sure, he's capable enough but he acts as if he's the only one on the road.'

Within hours of your arrival, you will already have gathered that anything goes. Overtaking on the inside, chatting on mobile phones, shooting red lights and not wearing a seatbelt may be illegal but are all par for the course. It also seems to be a matter of honour to let rip a torrent of abuse at passing motorists who are driving just as badly as you are and to rev your engine to scare the wits out of pedestrians at crossings.

In addition to an unhealthy love of speed, Argentine drivers may drive with no headlights at night and occasionally on the wrong side of the road. When one participant in a newspaper survey was asked 'When is it permissible to overtake on the inside?' (this is illegal in Argentina) his response was 'When you're in a hurry!' Disrespect for traffic laws can be quite shocking for the newcomer.

I experienced Argentine road etiquette firsthand when I caught a lift with Jesus and his nephew Angel in the rugged northwest. Jesus had a large truck and was charitably taking any hitchhikers who were also heading to Salta, piled in the back with peaches and massive hunks of goat's cheese. The trip was going swimmingly (we'd only had a handful of close shaves with oncoming vehicles and precipices) when a police road block loomed into view. As if on cue, all the drivers in the cars in front automatically reached for their seatbelts. But Jesus, who until then had struck me as the law-abiding type, swerved off the road as if in a scene from *Thelma and Louise*, and continued down a dirt track beside a canal, adding an extra hour tO our journey.

'Why the detour?' I asked innocently.

'Oh,' said Jesus without hesitation. 'My licence plate has fallen off, the brakes aren't working, my back light's shot through, I have passengers in the back without a permit and I haven't paid my tax foR five years.'

And don't think it's just the men who have no concept of the highway code. I've seen a woman driver fearlessly cut across six lanes of traffic after spotting her best friend on the sidewalk.

WOMEN

Across Argentina, but particularly in Buenos Aires, women are groomed and coifed to perfection. Meticulous in her appearance, the Argentine woman always seeks to make the most of herself and avidly follows the latest fashions in Paris, Milan and New York. Her international reputation for beauty is well deserved. To be honest, most Argentine women wouldn't look out of place on the catwalk.

Understandably, she simply adores shopping, which she does frequently with her large number of female friends. She is also a huge fan of the hairdressers, dropping in at least once a week to be blow-dried and manicured (as do many Argentine men).

Clothes are very important; there is a popular saying that an Argentine woman dresses up for other women and undresses for men.

Photo: Jamie Grant

Groomed and immaculate, three friends meet for tea.

As a woman, walking down the street you are just as likely to get eyeballed by other women checking out your clothes as by men checking out what's inside them.

An Argentine woman's most powerful weapon may well be her mascara wand, but this does not mean that she assumes the role of a second-class citizen. Back home it's clearly the women who rule the roost. (This can be seen in bars throughout the country when married men leap up and say, 'I've got to go home or my wife will kill me.') In their role as mother, Argentine women have attained a powerful, almost saint-like status at the centre of the all-important family. And young and old alike most assuredly know how to twist their men around their little finger, exercising every female wile in the book. It seems to come naturally from childhood.

They are also a smart, well-educated lot. University places are divided 50-50 between the sexes and women are already overtaking men in the medical profession. Unfortunately, however, while there are famous actresses and models, it is still rare for a woman to gain renown through business or politics. But on the stage and catwalk, they excel. Many Argentines including Valeria Mazza and Maria Ines Rivera grace the international catwalks and the covers of fashion magazines. Two of the greatest TV stars today in Argentina are women who host their own shows, command millions a year and make the rules for when and with whom they will appear. So, in spite of all the machismo undercurrents at work, it's probably not such a man's world after all.

Anorexics

Just as low fat yogurt is an Argentine woman's best friend, bulge is her greatest enemy. I don't think I have ever once seen any of my female Argentine friends eat the complimentary biscuit that arrived with their espresso, let alone bite into a chocolate bar without feeling awash with guilt. To put it bluntly, being fat in Argentina is socially unacceptable. Partly thanks to attitudes like this, Argentina is now in the unenviable position of topping the world charts for eating disorders. Experts are desperate to raise the alarm that the ever-increasing social pressure on Argentine women to be thin poses a serious threat to the nation's health.

At 20, my friend Veronica proudly boasts that she wears the same size jeans as when she was 14. That was at the height of her anorexia. Veronica has been on a string of strict diets since she was 11 – her 7-year-old cousin is on a diet at the moment – and she used to gobble down diet pills that she bought from the chemist. 'They made me feel bad, they messed up my head and gave me insomnia,' she says. But that didn't stop her from taking them. Veronica pats her thigh and says she needs to go on another diet again soon, that she's getting fat. But she is so thin that at times she looks like she'd snap in two.

Veronica is a typical everyday victim of the huge and unfair pressure on women to be beautiful and, more importantly, thin in Argentina. Some blame this on a macho society were women are judged primarily on their looks. Others blame it on the general

Argentine obsession with appearance. (A recent survey revealed that the main ambition of two-thirds of Argentine schoolgirls is to become a model.)

'We live in a very materialist culture with superficial values,' psychologist Paula Morinigo said. 'One in every four advertisements mention the body, everything is to do with diets and it's all very easy to get hold of.' Just walking around any town in Argentina, you'll be bombarded with advertisements promising the key to a perfect body. Supermarket shelves are stacked with diet products; laxatives and slimming pills are selling like hot cakes in pharmacies, and these days if you order a coke in one of Buenos Aires' famous cafés, chances are (if you're female) you'll be asked, 'Will that be Diet Coke?'

'In Argentina people just assume all girls are on a diet. Everyone is constantly talking about new diets and how much and what they eat,' says my friend Anna, a 23-year-old university student, and herself a former bulimic. 'When you get on a bus in Buenos Aires all the other girls eye you up and down, it's like a competition as to who is the thinnest or most beautiful and here you can only be beautiful if you are thin.'

This pressure isn't just on adolescents and young women – the traditional victims of eating disorders – but is also increasingly being felt by men (12 per cent of patients treated in Buenos Aires' clinics for eating disorders are male), older women and small children.

'Even young children are worried about their appearance,' says Dr Mabel Bello of the *Asociacion de Lucha contra Bulimia y Anorexia*. 'If you ask a school kid what do you want to be when you grow up, they'll answer, "thin".' Dr Bello has treated patients as young as 5 and 6 years old with severe bulimia and anorexia at her clinic in downtown Buenos Aires. 'In these cases there has usually been pressure from the family with a severe body culture. Some parents even put artificial sweetener in their baby's food.'

Such an alarmingly obsession with dieting couldn't have happened in a more unsuitable country. People love to socialise in

Argentina and practically every social occasion involves food, be it the Sunday barbecue or dinner with friends over an enormous bowl of pasta at the local Italian. So how on earth do you manage to resist Argentina's famously delicious food, I asked my skinny friends. 'Oh, we smoke and drink *mate.*'

Plastic Surgeons and Personal Trainers

If they're not starving or smoking themselves thin, many Argentine women may put themselves through gruelling exercise regimes in their quest to escape the dreaded spread. Television advertisements sell all sorts of hideous looking contraptions that promise to improve your physique. One – was it for a chastity belt? – bragged that it could make your bottom look 'nice and pert, just how men like it'.

In the ongoing quest to be body beautiful, many Argentines have resorted to the surgeon's knife, to nip and tuck, augment and reduce their various body parts, including, so they say, footballer Diego Maradona and former President Carlos Menem. The latter, at least, had the political sense to tell the nation that the giveaway bruising was from a nasty wasp sting.

Plastic surgery isn't the exclusive field of Argentina's rich and famous. Special summer deals, payment by interest-free instalments and reduced rates if you have more than one operation mean that plastic surgery is available to just about anyone who really wants it that badly. Just when I thought I had become immune to all the jutting cheekbones, hip bones and collagen-enhanced lips on the streets of Buenos Aires, I had my own mini culture shock when three lovely blonde sisters told me they'd all been given breast implants as 21st birthday presents from their mother!

If the surgeon's knife is too much to stomach, personal fitness trainers are now very much in vogue, especially among the *farándula* – Argentina's 'in' crowd of TV stars, models and playboys. You can hardly blame them. The *farándula* come under permanent scrutiny from the weekly gossip magazines whose headlines frequently read something along the lines of 'Moira/Susana/Graciela is looking fabulous, having lost 10 kilos in a fortnight' or (*gasp!*) 'so-and-so has let herself go' – a heinous crime in Argentina.

The Mothers and Grandmothers of the Plaza de Mayo

Just when you're starting to think you're in Beverly Hills rather than South America, you'll suddenly be brought down to earth with a shocking jolt. An article in a newspaper, something on television or even a passing flash of graffiti as your taxi races round a corner reminds you that Argentina has also lived through some dreadful dark days. If you're in Buenos Aires on a Thursday afternoon this reminder becomes even more poignant with the presence of a group of elderly women in the Plaza de Mayo.

At first sight, you might think these women are merely out for an afternoon stroll, but then you notice that they're all wearing white scarves on their heads, some are wearing badges, and they are holding placards with photos of young men or women. These photos are of their children and underneath is written the desperate plea, 'Where are they now?' Their children are the 'disappeared', some of the thousands of Argentines who were tortured and killed or just simply disappeared during the *Proceso* – a time when the military government declared an all-out 'Dirty War' against people they considered subversives.

These are Argentina's best-known mothers, gutsy, tough and fearless women who have taken on successive military and democratic governments in their search for truth and justice. They are known as 'the Mothers of the Plaza de Mayo' and have performed this weekly ritual since 1977, when a group of women first converged on the Plaza de Mayo to demand the whereabouts of their disappeared children and call for their murderers to be brought to justice. Their pain must be immeasurable, yet the mothers have never faltered in their demands and the search for their children and loved ones, even when faced with government threats and intimidation. As you can well imagine, the mothers are held in high regard in Argentina and their unceasing protests have come to represent the national conscience for the atrocities of the Dirty War.

I met one of the mothers, Margarita Peralta Gropper, in their office in Buenos Aires. 'I'm not in the house very often on my own, but when I am that's when I start to think about my poor boy and of the torture. It makes me sick,' said Margarita, whose son disappeared in 1977 when he was abducted from their house in Buenos Aires and taken away, she believes, to a clandestine torture centre.

'I couldn't do anything there, they took my son away and I couldn't get him back or ask for him, nothing. If he'd been in a police station or somewhere we knew I could have done something, but there, with the army, I was helpless and so was my son.'

Like so many innocent victims killed during the Dirty War, Margarita says her son was not even politically active. 'To this day I still don't know why they took him away. Sure he knew about politics as much as the rest of us but he didn't have any political affiliations, he just wanted to help everybody. He was everybody's friend, the best *compañero*.'

For Margarita, as for thousands of other mothers, it soon became clear that her son was never going to reappear alive. 'After an investigation told us that all the disappeared were presumed dead, my husband went white and grabbed his chest. Five days later he was dead,' said Margarita. 'Many other parents committed suicide or died. They didn't die of illness, they died out of desperation.'

The families of the disappeared know full well that many of the torturers still walk the streets and go unpunished, thanks to the general amnesty that had acquitted those involved in *El Proceso*. But the Mothers of the Plaza de Mayo have an ace up their sleeves. The amnesty laws which had left them powerless to touch their children's murderers did not cover the illegal adoption of the victims' babies, their grandchildren. Many of the disappeared women had been pregnant when they were seized by the military during the *Proceso*;

they had given birth before being executed. It is believed that more than a hundred babies were born into captivity and that many of these children had been illegally adopted, often by military families and their friends. Since 1983, a branch of the mothers has emerged known as 'the Grandmothers of the Plaza de Mayo'. These women are now using DNA testing in an attempt to trace their grandchildren and return them to their biological families.

PSYCHOANALYSTS

Argentines, *porteños* in particular, tend to spend a disproportionate amount of their spare time – and money – probing their psyches on the analyst's couch. Maybe such an addiction to therapy is an understandable offshoot of having lived through such atrocious times, of disappearances, torture and military governments. But psychoanalysis has actually been popular in Argentina since the 1960s, long before the Dirty War.

Today in Buenos Aires there are reputedly more psychoanalysts per capita than anywhere else in the world, and three times more than in New York state! Curious about such a startling statistic, it wasn't long before I started to make inquiries and was astonished to discover that nearly everybody I came across in Buenos Aires was in therapy for various and mysterious reasons. Even the psychoanalysts I met saw psychoanalysts, and trade unions and industrial organisations frequently look upon psychotherapy as an essential part of employees' benefit package.

One of my flatmates fell in love with his psychoanalyst and the subsequent break-up with her was so traumatic that he booked six months of sessions with another psychoanalyst. My flatmate, like most of my other friends in therapy, was permanently strapped for cash. Yet it appeared that he'd literally rather go without food than skip a session. 'If you're sick, you don't think twice about paying to see a doctor,' he told me. 'So why shouldn't we go and see our psychoanalysts when we've got problems?'

No one is in any way ashamed or tries to hide the fact that they are seeing a 'shrink'. On the contrary, a weekly visit to your psychoanalyst is considered the most natural thing in the world – rather like going to the hairdresser. You can't help feeling that having a psychoanalyst is something of a status symbol, rather like having a personal trainer.

As a result of this national obsession, conversations with your Argentine friends may be peppered with psychobabble: *trauma, oral fixation, according to my psychoanalyst* frequently pop up. Friends may discuss the merits of various treatments and swap names and addresses of their psychoanalysts. If you don't want to feel left out, try getting to grips with the works of Freud and Jacques Lacan, the main texts used among Argentina's psychoanalysts. Better still, if you really want to throw yourself into the culture, get your own psychoanalyst. You'll be spoilt for choice.

In the fierce competition, many psychoanalysts have sought to specialise. One newspaper carried an advertisement for a Christian psychoanalyst whose bold claim was that he'd read the bible. Another advertisement aimed to corner the gringo market by offering counselling for foreigners 'having problems adapting to life in Argentina'.

Whether all this psychoanalysis is a 'chicken or egg' thing or a profound problem with the Argentine psyche, nobody's too sure. But psychology students at least – and there are many in Argentina – know that they're on to a good thing.

'Why are so many Argentines addicted to psychoanalysis?' I asked Dr Jorge Garzareli, one of Buenos Aires' leading psychoanalysts. 'I think it's because of our origins. We come from all over the world and grew up very fast. We're still trying to get information about our roles in society and find our place in the world.'

MRS JONES' CREAM TEAS

Argentina's immigrant legacy never fails to turn up fascinating histories and anecdotes, yet it is undoubtedly at its most bizarre in the Patagonian province of Chubut where, in 1865, the good ship *Mimosa* docked at Puerto Madryn and deposited 160 Welsh men and women on the shores of southern Argentina. In their quest to get away from the English, these enterprising Welsh had wound up in the isolated wastes of Patagonia, at that time utterly barren and still inhabited by bands of Tchuclche Indians. (Even today, Chubut is probably further enough away from anywhere to have escaped the lure of psychoanalysis and plastic surgery.) As they moved westward in search of arable farming land, the colonisers settled in villages and towns which they christened with Welsh names such as Gaimán, Rawson, Dolavon and Trelew. They were soon joined by 3,000 more Welsh immigrants, effectively creating what Welsh minister Michael D. Jones dubbed 'a little Wales beyond Wales'.

Today, about 20,000 descendants of these early colonisers live in Argentina. Among them is Mrs Mirna Jones who serves up sumptuous cream teas to visiting tourists in her parlour at Ty Nain in Gaimán.

Mrs Jones' spread includes apple pie, lemon meringue, pumpkin jam, a decadent Black Forest gateaux and tea served in the best china pots. The walls and tables of her tea parlour are covered with Welsh memorabilia and lace tablecloths, and a gramophone and an old

Mrs Jones reminisces about her Welsh ancestors in her tea parlour in Gaimán.

church organ stand against a wall. Outside, rose bushes brave the Patagonian wind, clinging to the stonewalled cottage with sash windows that looks as if it has been directly transplanted from the real Welsh countryside.

'We don't just sell tea,' Mrs Jones told me in between bites of scones smothered in her delicious home-made marmalade, 'we sell tradition.' I think she was having a subtle dig at some of the new teahouses that have sprung up in the area, cashing in on the exotic appeal of tucking into Welsh cream teas in Patagonia. Mrs Jones, however, is the genuine article. She looks Welsh and, even though she has never actually been to Wales, knows how to speak Welsh. 'If we spoke Spanish to my grandparents they refused to answer us,' she remembers. But when it comes down to it, Mirna Jones has no doubts whatsoever as to her identity. 'We are Argentines. Our roots may be from somewhere else, but we definitely feel 100 per cent Argentine.'

OTHER LATIN AMERICANS

There's no doubt that Argentina is a country of immigrants from the Joneses of Patagonia to the Russian Jewish community of Buenos Aires. Yet a more recent wave of newcomers continues to pour into Argentina from neighbouring Latin American countries. These immigrants, mainly from Bolivia, Peru, Paraguay and Chile, have come seeking work and a better life. Many of them, however, end up doing backbreaking work for little pay and live in miserable conditions. Tens of thousands, if not millions (statistics, understandably, are hard to come by), of non-Argentine Latin Americans now live and work illegally in Argentina. With their indigenous and mestizo looks that so easily differentiate them from the majority of Argentines, they have become easy targets for racism and are often blamed for escalating violence and for taking work away from Argentines. The truth is that most of these immigrants work the black market and remain largely excluded from the system. Often, they are even admired for their hard work ethic and for doing the type of jobs – such as shoeshining, plumbing and digging drains – that many Argentines would rather not do.

Ironically, although many of these immigrants lack civil and political rights, sometimes working in slave-like conditions, when they are caught by the police or immigration authorities, they actually leap to the defence of their bosses. When 45 undocumented Bolivian women, working 15–18 hour shifts in a clothing factory, were discovered by the authorities, they all spoke up for their employer, despite the fact that they had been forced to sleep on mattresses on the workshop floor and forbidden to leave the building. In Argentina they were earning 200 dollars a month, a small fortune by standards back home in Bolivia. For now, Argentina still holds the magic of a country where they can make their fortune.

Many of the new immigrant arrivals live in the *villas miserias*, or shantytowns on the fringes of Argentina's cities, alongside many poor Argentine migrants from the provinces attracted by the hope of finding work in service and manufacturing industries. Some say that Argentina is too rich and too white to be considered Third World. Well, a visit to a *villa* – with its drop latrines, precarious housing, unpaved streets and pervading atmosphere of violence and crime – would soon change their minds.

THE POLICE

Few of the country's policemen even dare to enter the *villas miserias*, not that they'd have much success in catching any of the villains that seek refuge inside. 'The secret of survival is that you don't know anything, that you haven't seen anything,' said one inhabitant of a *villa* in an interview. 'The sneaks pay with their life.'

Even outside the *villas*, the average policeman on the street tends to be widely mistrusted by the public and this perception isn't helped by the fact that they have gained a rather trigger-happy reputation. Many Argentines don't even bother to report crimes, believing at best that nothing will get resolved or at worst that the police themselves might be involved. Still, it can't be much fun being a policeman in Argentina. Armed shootouts are an increasingly common occurrence and many policemen hold down two jobs, working as private guards on the side to supplement their meagre salary of about US$400 a month. Others get paid under the table to patrol a certain area or 'earn' extra money through bribes. Frequently, a neighbourhood may club together to hire a private security guard – as clear a sign as any of a lack of faith in effectual policing.

HEROES AND VILLAINS

Following is a guide to Argentina's famous and infamous 20th century sons and daughters – from TV stars to writers, politicians and musicians. (Key historical figures are dealt with in Chapter 1.) Armed with this information, you will hopefully be able to hold your own in conversation, keep up with the gossip and bluff your way through dinner parties.

Raúl Alfonsín: President from 1983 to 1989 and the first democratically elected leader since the return to democracy. Alfonsín, from the Radical Party, put many top-ranking military leaders in jail and set up a commission to investigate the disappearances under *El Proceso*. However, his administration was plagued with economic problems and hyperinflation, and he resigned several months before the end of his term.

Jorge Luis Borges: 1899–1986, Argentina's greatest literary hero, novelist, poet and essayist, whose works include the *Universal History of Infamy, Fictions, El Aleph* and *Dr Brodie's Report*. A classic Anglo-Argentine, Borges was brought up in 'a garden, behind speared railings and in a library of limitless English books' and had the speech and manners of an Edwardian gentleman. A virulent anti-*peronista*, Perón 'promoted' him from chief librarian to inspector of poultry. In later life he was blind. He died, aged 87, in Geneva where he is buried.

José Luis Cabezas: Photojournalist for *Noticias* magazine whose handcuffed charred corpse was found in January 1997 inside a burnt rental car near the coastal resort of Pinamar in Buenos Aires province. He was believed to have been murdered under the orders of **Alfredo Yabrán**, a shady mafioso-type character with fingers in many pies, who allegedly controlled postal services, airports, judges and cabinet ministers. Yabrán blew his head off with a shotgun in his mansion in Entre Ríos minutes before the police moved in to arrest him. Or did he? No one's too sure. Some say he may have been murdered, others that he's still alive, living under a new alias. The mystery continues...

Julio Cortázar: 1914–84, arguably Argentina's most famous and most prolific 20th century novelist, whose books include *Los Premios*, *Rayuela* (Hopscotch), and *Queremos tanto a Glenda*. He wrote many of his novels in exile and was greatly influenced by James Joyce.

Fernando De la Rua: A former mayor of Buenos Aires and leader of the Alliance Party who was elected president in 1999, winning almost 50 per cent of the vote and ending 10 years of *peronist* rule. He himself admits that he's boring. De la Rua has vowed to clamp down on corruption and stick to the free-market reforms.

Juan Manuel Fangio: Formula One car racer, five times champion in the 1950s and arguably one of Argentina's best sportsmen. Fangio led a scandal-free life, kept a low profile and was a true gentleman. He died in 1995 and remains an idol.

Martín Fierro: Argentina's most famous (fictional) gaucho created by José Hernández in his epic poem of the same name. Practically every Argentine possesses a well-thumbed copy of this classic.

Leopoldo Galtieri: General who invaded Falkland Islands and head of the military junta from December 1981 to June 1982, now widely dismissed as a drunk. Galtieri is presently under house arrest for his involvement in the illegal adoption of babies during *El Proceso*.

Charly Garcia: Eccentric grizzled rock hero with a trademark black-and-white moustache whose gravelly voice still drives audiences wild. Thoroughly anti-establishment youth hero.

Carlos Gardel: Undoubtedly the greatest tango singer of all time, as well as an aspiring actor and a national hero. Never seen without his trilby and heart-stopping smile. When he died in 1935 in a plane crash many Argentines felt orphaned. His well-visited tomb in Chacarita cemetery is covered with plaques and flowers and a larger-than-life-size statue of 'the songbird of Buenos Aires'.

Susana Giménez: Impossibly chiselled TV diva and chat show hostess, with metres of platinum blonde hair and Zsa Zsa Gabor's eyes. She is widely adored throughout the country and her show *Hola Susana* gets huge ratings.

Ernesto 'Che' Guevara, Argentina's prodigal son.

Ernesto 'Che' Guevara: Sexy 60s revolutionary who wore combat trousers and a beret and smoked cigars. Guevara was born in Rosario in 1928 and grew up in Córdoba where he studied medicine at the university. He became Castro's right hand in the Cuban revolution before being shot dead at the age of 39 in the Bolivian mountains trying to foment worldwide revolution. Still a big icon among Argentine students.

Mirtha Legrand: Susana's arch-rival, Mirtha is older and arguably more sophisticated. Housewives adore her show *Lunching with Mirtha Legrand*.

75

Mafalda: Cheeky comic cartoon girl who is always asking questions and spouting her views on humanity. Mafalda, who loves the Beatles and hates soup, was created by the comic genius **Quino** in 1964 and has become both a top Argentine personality and something of a national heroine.

Diego Maradona: The *enfant terrible* and national hero of Argentina's football scene, Maradona grew up in Villa Fiorito, a shantytown on the outskirts of Buenos Aires. By the age of 15, he was playing in premier division matches for Argentinos Juniors. He later played for Boca Juniors, Barcelona and Napoli FCs. His greatest moment came in the 1986 World Cup in Mexico – where he earned the title of the most talented footballer the world had ever seen. In 1994, he tested positive in a dope test during the US World Cup. Yet in Argentina public sympathy remains with Maradona.

Carlos Saul Menem: President from 1989 to 1999, the flamboyant former governor of La Rioja has been described as the president who doesn't give a damn if Argentines laugh at him. With big hair (he once wore a toupee), elaborate sideburns and an equally eye-catching smile, Menem likes playing football, flying, fast cars and beautiful women. The entire nation was gripped by his very public divorce – at one stage he had his wife Zulema evicted from the presidential residence after a tiff. Despite being a *peronist*, he opened up the market economy and introduced a wide-sweeping privatisation plan.

Carlos Monzón: Heavyweight boxing champion whose life was struck by tragedy. Monzón murdered his wife and died in a car crash shortly after being paroled from prison.

Fito Paez: Rock soloist from Rosario whose albums include *Tercer Mundo*, *El Amor Despues el Amor* and *Circo Beat*. Even the uninitiated listener will be drawn to his unique style.

Patoruzú: A much-loved cartoon character created by Dante Quinterno, Patoruzú first appeared in a comic strip in the 1930s and has been charming generations of Argentines ever since. Modelled on a Patagonian Indian with superhuman powers and a heart of gold, he is never seen without Pampero, his beloved horse, or Isodoro, his *porteño* (and *vivo*) sidekick.

Juan Domingo Perón: Undoubtedly the biggest name in Argentine politics, Perón rose to power on the back of a military coup in 1943 and was elected to the presidency three times. Despite his death in 1974, *peronismo* has remained a driving force in Argentine politics.

Eva 'Evita' Perón: General Perón's glamorous mistress and, later, wife. Evita is one of the most loved – and reviled – figures of Argentina's 20th century. She died of cancer in 1952, at the age of 33. Her name has become even more internationally famous since the release of the musical and later the movie *Evita* with Madonna in the title role.

Astor Piazzolla: Tango musician and composer born in Argentina to Italian parents. Piazzolla spent much of his childhood in New York and is widely credited (and occasionally attacked) for bringing tango into modern times with jazz and classical fusions. He died in 1992.

Gabriela Sabatini: Tennis star and sexy brunette who wowed spectators at Wimbledon and other international tournaments – and it wasn't just her forehand! Now retired from professional tennis, Sabatini is an astute businesswoman with a flourishing perfume business.

Mercedes Sosa: Folkloric singer and much-loved motherly figure with an incredibly powerful voice, she performs tear-jerking renditions of South American classics.

Marcelo Tinelli: TV star and for the last decade Argentina's most popular entertainer. He is the handsome and funny host of *Videomatch*.

Jorge Rafael Videla: Protagonist of the 1976 coup and first leader of the military junta. He was succeeded by General **Roberto Viola** in 1981, who in turn was replaced by **Galtieri**. Videla and other military officers were imprisoned in 1983 but pardoned by Menem. He is now facing charges of kidnapping and the illegal adoption of babies during *El Proceso*.

Virgin of Luján: Argentina's patron saint is also more affectionately known as *la Virgencita*. Legend has it that in 1630 a wagon with a painting of the Virgin en route from Brazil wouldn't move until the painting was removed. And there it stayed at what is now the town of Luján. The Virgin is now housed in Luján's basilica and visited by 4 million pilgrims a year. It is said that she has appeared in visions on numerous occasions to many Argentines.

Chapter Four

SOCIAL CUSTOMS

'Reveller!
Dammit, you're such fun.
Reveller!
A wasted man you are.'

—From the tango *Garufa* (1928),
lyrics by Roberto Fontaina and Victor Solino

The problem with adapting to life in Argentina is that sometimes it looks so familiar, you start to act as you would back home. So you go out to eat supper at a respectable 8:00 pm, but none of the restaurants have even opened yet. You've been stood up for an important engagement because there's been an unexpected snowfall and everybody you want to do business with is off skiing in Bariloche. People light up cigarettes in the supermarket queue in front of you without the slightest compunction and you just don't understand why you can't get a cup of coffee to take away.

The key here is to be open-minded, to expect the unusual and go along with it. Before you know it you'll find it impossible to believe that you ever drank *decaf* or went to bed before midnight.

GOING OUT

It's social suicide to be seen in a bar before midnight, and in a nightclub before two. Argentines go out as late as possible and stay out as late as possible. In fact, the later you arrive and the later you stay, the more fashionable you are. You'll soon discover that there's something delightfully decadent in partying till dawn, staying out for breakfast and frequently heading straight on to work. For weeks, I thought my Buenos Aires *barrio* was rather quiet and then I realised that nine in the evening was far too early for the local night owls – the place was absolutely heaving with party-goers at three in the morning.

A word of warning. Don't think you can get away with the occasional late Friday or Saturday night, relying on Sunday to recover. Weekends, unofficially, start early here. The conventional weekend isn't enough for the Argentine party animal. Thursday night is generally considered the start of the weekend as regards going out until you drop, and this is frequently being pulled back now to Wednesday (even though both Thursday and Friday it is work as usual). If you do try and 'flake out' of going out you'll find little sympathy among your companions. You'll simply be told to *ponete las pilas* – put the batteries in – and join in the fun.

My first night on the tiles in Buenos Aires began around two in the morning. I'd given up any thoughts of going out when 12 o'clock chimed and my hostess was still in her pyjamas nonchalantly eating ravioli. 'Bah,' I thought, 'these *porteños* are all talk and no do. They're not the party animals I've been led to believe.' I couldn't have been more wrong. Like Cinderella's wilder sister, when two o'clock struck my hostess leapt up, threw on a gold lamé dress and hailed a passing cab to take us to a multistorey disco where we danced until seven in the morning.

And don't think that it's just the Capital Federal with the bright lights. Country folk they may be elsewhere, but when it comes to going out they're just as wild as their friends in the city, frequently worse. In fact, staying up all night is so common, Argentines tend to talk in terms of the 24-hour clock (otherwise a meeting at one o'clock might be a lunch date or a disco date) and they've even adopted a word to describe someone who stays up all night – *trasnochador*.

FLIRTING

One of the main reasons the Argentines love to go out so much is that it provides them with the perfect opportunity to indulge in their favourite national pastime: flirting. Argentines, both men and women, are fantastic flirts. Most everyday transactions, whether it's a quick visit to the local kiosk or buying the morning newspaper, will involve a certain amount of flirting. The butcher who hands your *bife* to you over the counter may do so with a wink or a raised eyebrow and the waitress who brings your coffee might catch your eye and hold it for just that little bit longer. The Argentine word for flirt, *coqueta*, however, can only apply to women. Argentine men will staunchly deny that they flirt, but they do.

Rodolfo, a flirtatious chef from La Plata, explained the situation to me: 'Women flirt, men don't. Men show off.' He continued: 'If I'm in a bar and I see a girl I like, it doesn't matter one bit if she doesn't show any interest in me, because that's when I begin to show off. First, I have to catch her eye and try to speak to her. She will, of course, ignore me (otherwise she is seen as easy). I will insist. If she carries on playing hard to get, I will begin to lie; I'll tell her about my

Mercedes Benz, my great city job and so on. I will only give up if my advances are rejected five or six times and then I can't show my face in that bar again for weeks.'

'The problem,' adds Rodolfo after much thought, 'is that women think that we men are only interested in sex.'

The truth is, to a certain degree, Argentines are very much interested in sex. You only have to stroll through a shopping mall or switch on the TV to realise that sex sells in Argentina. Advertisements are saturated with beautiful and often scantily clad women, while those promoting products tend to employ impossibly glamorous girls dressed in minuscule miniskirts to hand out leaflets and free product samples. Nevertheless, flirting is always done in the best possible taste in Argentina, and it is largely an end in itself rather than a means to an end.

GREETING PEOPLE

Unless they're behind the wheel of a car, Argentines are some of the friendliest people on earth and greetings will generally be warm and effusive. Women kiss women, men kiss women, and men, if they know each other well, will also kiss other men. This is usually one kiss on the right cheek for both sexes. However, your first man-to-man meeting will probably begin with a hearty handshake.

The man-to-man kiss may come as a shock to many a male visitor to Argentina unaccustomed to bristly kisses. 'The first time my friend kissed me was awful,' said Alfredo, a Brazilian working in Buenos Aires. 'I was like, no no no, I'm not a homosexual. Then I realised that everyone did it.'

As a rule, if you enter a room you are to kiss everybody hello and as you leave you repeat the entire process and kiss everybody goodbye. If this is confusing, then lose your street cred and be the first to arrive and the last to leave. Then you'll be the receiver of all the kisses rather than the protagonist. The same rules apply if you bump into a friend on the street. You kiss him/her hello, then you must kiss everyone who is with your friend hello, and they in turn kiss all of your friends hello as well, even if none of them have ever met before!

In Argentina, you should never approach a stranger for information without first greeting that person with a *buenos días* (good morning), *buenas tardes* (good afternoon) or *buenas noches* (good evening). The same applies if you walk into a shop or a restaurant.

Finally, in the countryside and small villages it is customary to greet all those you pass on the road, even if you've never laid eyes on them before in your life. Obviously, for practical reasons at least, this is not done in cities or larger towns.

To 'Vos' Or Not To 'Vos'

Argentines can be quite informal and relaxed when addressing others. With people their own age or contemporaries they generally use the informal *vos* (the Argentine equivalent of the Spanish second person singular *tu* – meaning 'you') straight away, rather than the formal *usted* (you). Elders, business associates and people in important or bureaucratic positions, however, should be addressed as *usted*. If you are unsure of what to say, play it safe with *usted* until you are invited to use the informal expression.

Informal they may be, but in the appropriate setting Argentines can be extremely title-conscious. University graduates may be addressed as *Licenciado*. Engineers are addressed as *Ingeniero* and architects are *Arquitecto*. Lawyers and doctors and PhDs are all addressed as *Doctor*. But people who are quite clearly neither PhD grads nor medical doctors may also be called *Doctor*. This is meant out of respect so don't make life difficult by asking exactly what they are a doctor of.

Che, Don't Call Me That!

Argentines are great fans of hoisting nicknames onto everyone they meet. Even as a foreigner, you will be no exception. This has the immediate effect of making life a lot more personal, which is how people like it. There is, however, one universal nickname which locals and visitors to Argentina will be called all the time – *Che*. It's practically impossible to give a literal translation of *Che*, it's something like 'buddy' or 'friend' or just 'hey you'. Even its origins are murky, but it is generally believed to be a derivation of the Mapuche Indian word for 'people'.

Your waiter can be called *Che*, so can your best friend, your taxi driver or just someone walking by of whom you want to ask the time. *Che* knows no class or sex boundaries. You just are. Often *Che* is preceded by the exclamation *Oye*! to get someone's attention.

Thanks to the wide use of this word in Argentina, the Argentines as a race are often simply referred to as *Los Ches*. This is in fact how the Argentine-Cuban revolutionary Ernesto 'Che' Guevara got his nickname.

There are, however, many variations on the *Che* theme. You may be called *amigo* (friend) or *hermano* (brother). If you look Chinese, you could be called *chino*; if dark-skinned or black, you may be called *negro*. I know of one man who had large bushy eyebrows and was known as *cejudo* – the eyebrowed one – by his friends. For years Diego Maradona with his trademark flowing locks was known as *El Pelusa*, the straggly-haired one. If you're bald or have very short hair you might be known as *pelado* (baldy). If you're on the larger side you might get called *chancho* (piggy) or *gordo* (fatty). And if you're thin you'll be called *flaco* (skinny). Old people may be referred to as *viejo*, although probably not directly to their faces unless they are your parents – who will take it as a sign of affection. Most letters home in Argentina open with '*Queridos Viejos*', which is the equivalent of writing to your parents and opening with the rather curious greeting, 'My Dear Oldies'.

All this may seem shockingly racist, 'sizeist', 'ageist' and 'looksist' but no insult is meant at all, and strange as it may seem, it's actually meant affectionately. If you react with outrage to your new nickname, you'll simply be greeted with half-amused curiosity.

You should also take your nickname with a large pinch of salt. *Gordo* (fatty), for example, is frequently used as a term of endearment between husbands and wives, even if they are *flaco*. If the nickname is rounded off with an *–ito* on the end, then it's meant even more endearingly. *Gordo* becomes *gordito* (little fat one), *flaco – flaquito* (little skinny one) and so on. Even your real name can take on this diminutive: if your name is Carlos, you could be known as *Carlitos*.

Then there are the double nicknames that combine *Che* with a more personalised name – *Che flaco, Che gordo, Che Carlitos* and so on. The combinations are mind-boggling.

Understandably, this degree of name-calling can play havoc with your self-image. 'If someone calls me *gordita,* however endearingly, I hate them and swear to go on a diet,' confided an Australian friend who was thin even by *porteño* standards. 'But if they call me *flaca*, I'm on an immediate high and happily gorge myself on ice cream.'

(*Note:* For women, the 'o' at the end is substituted with an 'a', thus *amigo* becomes *amiga*, *flaquito* becomes *flaquita* and so on. *Che*, however, is always *Che*, whatever your sex.)

MARRIAGE AND LOVE AFFAIRS

Like most social functions in Argentina, weddings start late and end late. Wedding jitters must be extra-exacerbated because the church ceremony usually takes place as late as 8:00 or 9:00 pm. This means that the wedding feast doesn't start until 10 to 11-ish and in some cases as late as midnight. The party proper, with live bands and dance floor, kicks off in the small hours. How they have energy for the honeymoon is anyone's guess!

Children tend to live with their *viejos* until they get married, then they live with their spouses and new family. Bachelor pads exist but they are an exception rather than the rule. As is 'living in sin', which remains a social taboo. This does not mean that all Argentines remain chaste until their wedding night. *Albergue transitorios* (hotels that rent rooms out by the hour) provide for young lovers, for those having

Photo: Jamie Grant

A romantic tryst in Puerto Madero.

affairs (Argentina is said to have the highest infidelity rate in the whole of South America) and even for happily married couples looking for some privacy.

Divorce has been legal in Argentina since 1987, and now Argentina also claims South America's highest divorce rate. Divorcees, however, can't get remarried in a Catholic church.

THE FAMILY

As in most Latin countries, the family is the central pillar of Argentine life. As a result families tend to be large and extended and relations generally live nearby. Argentine children will probably grow up with cousins as some of their best friends. Children are especially adored in Argentina and few screaming kids are told to shut up – instead they are lovingly humoured and welcome absolutely everywhere and anytime. It's easy to see how Argentines get into the habit of staying up late at an early age. It's also perfectly normal for complete

Photo: Jamie Grant

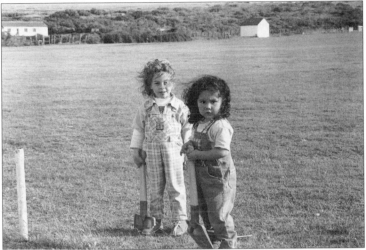

Two cousins play together in Patagonia.

strangers to bestow oohs and ahhs on small children and ruffle their hair without being branded paedophiles!

Growing Up

Like their mothers, Argentina's youth are sleek, glossy and generally impeccably dressed. There's no awkward adolescence for these kids; instead they seem to ooze confidence from a young age and are remarkably relaxed and chatty. One of the greatest social delights in Argentina is the complete ease with which the young and old interact with each other.

Two key events mark children's lives as they grow up. For girls, it is their 15th birthday or *quincena,* an important landmark to celebrate the end of girlhood and the transformation into a young woman. Given half a chance, the *quincena* can rapidly turn into a huge social affair involving expensive dresses, photos and maybe a slot in a magazine's society gossip pages. Occasionally, the whole family will take a celebratory trip to Miami or Disneyland, but more often than not parents will throw a big party at home for their daughter, where she dresses up in white and is given a large cake that looks suspiciously like a wedding cake.

The other great excitement for Argentine teens is the riotous graduate trip (*viaje de egresados*). In this well-earned celebration for finishing high school, a large group of schoolfriends, or even the whole class, go on holiday together for about ten days.

Practically every *viaje de egresados* takes place in Bariloche, thanks to this city's proliferation of discos and perpetual holiday atmosphere. Most graduate trips take place in November, when school breaks up, but many students go in the July vacation before they've officially graduated, for the skiing. For many, this is the first time they've ever been skiing, so they throw themselves into it with reckless abandon. If you don't like crowds and you're not 18 years old, it's probably a good idea to avoid Bariloche at these times of the year.

FUN AND GAMES

Entertainment is enormously important to Argentines, who generally 'work to live' rather than 'live to work'. Dining out is one of the main forms of entertainment. Likewise, the Argentine 'lives to eat' rather than 'eats to live', but this will be discussed further in Chapter 6.

Street Life and El Paseo

In the ongoing quest to see and be seen, Argentines take to the streets in large numbers. Weather permitting, as much as possible takes place outdoors. Cafés spill out onto the pavements under colourful umbrellas. Sash windows of restaurants are flung open to invite in the breeze and admiring glances. Bored and glamorous secretaries loll out of balconies five floors up above the traffic. And if there is a common gripe, my goodness, you'll soon know about it! Thousands will take to the streets in protest, clang their saucepans on the balconies, beat drums and let off bangers in some of the most exciting (but largely peaceful) demonstrations you'll have seen in a long time.

With so much action going on outside, the streets become a key venue for campaigning politicians and businessmen. Cars with loud-speakers blare out music interspersed with announcements of new supermarkets or even lost pets. When things really hot up aeroplanes fly overhead and drop thousands of flyers onto the crowds down below. Street walls suddenly become ideal backdrops for murals and political propaganda. Political posters are layered on top of each other like wallpaper, and graffiti makes sure everyone knows exactly what everyone else thinks of the government.

But by far the most important outside event is *el paseo* (the stroll). In this respect, the Spanish plaza system, a relic from colonial times, is ideal. You can happily circle the plaza in one direction while the object of your desire circles in the other. In Patagonia, no doubt due to the plunging temperatures, *el paseo* takes place in cars, which drive round and round the town centre. No one gets the slightest bit embarrassed to be seen driving round in circles eyeing each other up. The aim, you must remember, is to see and to be seen.

Truco – The Subtle Art of Lying

It's a common sight to see duelling chess players engrossed over a game on a park bench or through a smoky café window. I'm quite convinced that the world's longest game of chess is taking place in a café in Buenos Aires. Every time I walk past the window, two men – utterly absorbed in their game – are bent over a chessboard in unwavering concentration. They've been there for so long that the waiters treat them as part of the furniture, casually moving them to one side as they sweep the floor. But if you think they take chess seriously, you should see the Argentines get immersed in a game of *truco*.

Truco is a card game played with Spanish cards (depicting swords, cups, wands and pentacles as opposed to clubs, spades, hearts and diamonds) that involves much wit, a certain amount of skill and a

Photo: Jamie Grant

A street artist adds a splash of colour to a Buenos Aires neighbourhood.

natural ability to lie. The Argentine trait of *viveza criolla* – or artful lying – really comes into its own in a *truco* game. If it is played in pairs, as is usual, you are required to make certain facial expressions so that your partner sitting opposite can guess what you have in your hand. For example, a twitching cheek means you have a seven, a raised eyebrow and you're holding an ace. If you purse your lips, as if blowing a kiss, you're probably holding a two. The real skill lies not so much in making the faces as in making them without the other pair seeing you. If they are watching closely, players may resort to playing footsie under the table, tapping messages across onto their partner's feet. Of course, all this is secondary to an ability to keep a poker face while lying through your teeth.

It will be well worth your while to learn how to play *truco* as long as you are in Argentina, although this is easier said than done. The rules are about as complicated and seemingly random as American football would be to an Englishman. Once you have learnt to play, however, you should not enter into a *truco* game lightly. *Truco* can be taken very seriously indeed and vast amounts of money have been known to change hands over games.

'Duck' and Other Gaucho Games

Lots of original gaucho games are still played today in Argentina, the most flamboyant of which is *pato*, a sort of basketball crossed with rugby. Naturally, it is played on horseback and at great speed.

In the original form of the game, a duck – *pato* in Spanish – was put in a basket and left at an equal distance from two encampments. Competing gaucho teams lined up and galloped towards it, the aim being to get possession of the duck and carry it home. Whoever got the duck first was frantically pursued by the opposing team, whose members would do anything to seize the duck, including lassoing opponents with *boleadores*, cutting saddles free and pulling men off their horses at full gallop. The game was considered so violent that in 1776 the Catholic Church threatened to excommunicate players.

Today *pato* has been toned down. Still, it's not exactly cricket. The hapless duck has long since been replaced by a large leather ball with six handles which is thrown, wrenched and passed between players on horseback who score goals by throwing it through a type of basketball hoop. The players may have swapped their sombreros and ponchos for American-style football helmets and leather kneepads but the spirit remains. If you're in luck you may be able to catch a *pato* game at an *estancia* or even at one of the *pato* tournaments in Buenos Aires.

Another popular gaucho game still played today is *sortija*, which is slightly reminiscent of a medieval jousting tournament. At full gallop and standing up in his stirrups, the mounted gaucho tries to aim a thin needle-like stick through a ring hanging from a pole. It requires incredible amounts of skill and superb horsemanship.

But if you really want to see the modern-day gauchos at their fearless best, try to get to a rodeo, known locally as a *doma*. Rodeos are held throughout the country.

Theatre and Cinema

When the dazzling Teatro Colón first opened its doors in 1908 with Verdi's *Aida*, a precedent was set for Argentina's arts scene. Designed by Italian architects with La Scala in mind, the lavishly decorated Colón takes up an entire block of central Buenos Aires. Inside, it is awash with red and gold trimmings, glittering chandeliers and exquisite sculptures, a grand reminder of Argentina's *belle epoch*. It is arguably the best opera house in Latin America and one of the greatest in the world. During the theatre season, which runs between April and December, an equally dazzling audience settle into plush velvet armchairs in the auditorium or stand shoulder-to-shoulder on top-floor balconies.

The Teatro Colón is the jewel in what is a very glittering crown. Argentines love to go out to the theatre and cinema and will do so as often as possible. A few blocks away from the palatial Colón is Corrientes Avenue. Dubbed the 'street that never sleeps', it is choca-bloc with theatres. A *porteño* saying holds that you can go to the theatre every night for a month in Buenos Aires and see a different show each time.

Argentines are equally fans of the cinema and Argentine film has gained international renown. It has also been one of the few avenues in which the atrocities of the Dirty War are aired. Don't miss Luis Puenzo's *La Historia Oficial* (The Official Version), in which a middle-class family comes to terms with the fact that its adopted daughter is the child of a disappeared victim kidnapped during the *Proceso*. It won an Oscar in 1986 for the best foreign film and attracted widespread international attention. Fernando Solanas' *Tangos, El Exilo de Gardel* (Tangos, the Exile of Gardel), explores the lives of those living in exile in Paris during the military dictatorship. Maria Luisa Bemberg's *Camila*, set 150 years earlier during the dictatorship of Juan Manuel de Rosas, retells the true story of Camila O'Gorman, the daughter of a wealthy creole landowner who fell in love with a priest and was eventually executed. The parallels of Rosas' days portrayed in the film – torture, state terrorism, dissidents' disappearance and liquidation – with the recent military dictatorship weren't lost on anyone when the film was released in 1984.

Argentine films are received with obvious anticipation by local audiences, but Hollywood blockbusters are also wildly popular. Come prepared, though, for a confusing stream of jazzed up Spanish titles. For example, Kenneth Brannagh's production of Shakespeare's *Much Ado About Nothing* went under the title of *Much Noise, Few Nuts*, while *The Sound of Music* played under the rather suggestive title of *The Rebel Nun*! Appealing to the Argentine sense of mischief, many other movie titles are loaded with lots more sexual or romantic innuendoes than the original English title lets on. In one week in Buenos Aires, they were showing what translated as the rather titillating *Forbidden Love*, *Sexual Games* and *The Other Face of Love* – these turned out to be the more innocent sounding *Cruel Intentions, A Destiny of Her Own* and *Chasing Amy*.

Meanwhile, bearing in mind the Argentine passion for late nights, it's not altogether uncommon to go to the cinema at two in the morning – look out for the *trasnoche* show.

(*Note:* Cinemas across the country have cheap days once a week, usually Wednesday, when ticket prices are slashed in half.)

Country Houses

Distances are vast in Argentina, and Argentines don't think twice about travelling for hours for lunch or a social call. Some *estancias* are so isolated that they have their own airstrips and petrol stations.

To combat this mileage problem, many *porteños* with the means to do so have sought out weekend cottages within 45 minutes' drive from downtown Buenos Aires. For convenience and safety, these *quintas* (country houses) are bunched together with other *quintas* in a secure enclosure. As one cynical commentator put it, 'Everybody who lives together in the same Buenos Aires neighbourhood leaves Buenos Aires on Friday night and goes to another neighbourhood, where they spend the weekend "getting away from it all" with the same people that they spent all week with.'

These countryside enclosures are known as country clubs, or simply *los countries*. Most have a communal swimming pool, tennis courts and a brace of polo pitches. Security is tight: the area is surrounded by a fence and a mean-looking armed guard is posted at the gate. Not any old José can buy up and move into a *country*; you have to have your name put forward by a member and even then you have to be socially accepted. A quiz in the daily *Clarin* newspaper revealed how to tell if you've been accepted by your *country*. 'Does the guard (A) greet you affectionately and throw open the barrier as you approach the gates or (B) warily approach your car, revolver in hand?' was one of the slightly tongue-in-cheek questions posed.

Country clubs and private barrios may be heavily armed and closed off to the general public but in the real countryside it's relatively easy to stroll up to any country house. Should you decide to drop in on the residents of such establishments, it is customary to clap your hands together a couple of times as you approach. Many houses have open courtyards and visitors are few and far between, so if you don't make your arrival known beforehand you could spring your hosts *in flagrante*, or worse still, get attacked by their miffed Rottweiler. Many older people may also call out '*Ave Maria Purissima*' when approaching a house in the countryside.

ANYONE FOR POLO?

Although polo didn't originate in Argentina, it is a sport that is unquestionably associated with the country and has been played here since 1875. Today, there are few polo teams in the world – good ones at least – that can't boast an Argentine player or two. Non-Argentines are invariably awestruck by the standard of Argentina's players, who, they joke, were probably born on a horse. It's not unusual to see small Argentine children fearlessly charging about on horseback clutching polo sticks while their contemporaries abroad have probably just mastered riding a bicycle. In fact, the local talent is so extensive that entire teams can be made up of brothers alone. (You can't help wickedly wondering if they were bred specifically for the purpose!)

Throughout the world, all polo players have a rating known as a handicap, which reflects their ability and can range from zero goals for a complete beginner (minus two outside Argentina) up to a

Playing polo on an estancia *in the pampas.*

maximum of ten goals for the very best players. Argentina, understandably, holds the monopoly on the very best players. To get some
idea of the Argentine talent, at the time of writing only 12 players in
the world are rated with a 10-goal handicap; eight of these are from
Argentina. One of Argentina's best teams – formed by the four
dashing Heguy brothers – had, at one stage, a combined handicap of
40 goals, the absolute highest any team can get.

The Argentine polo player is frequently stereotyped as devilishly
good-looking, devastatingly macho and usually to be seen with a
martini in one hand and an exquisite girlfriend in the other. Chances
are that he also rubs shoulders with Prince Charles and the Sultan of

Brunei and has sponsors like Cartier. I know I shouldn't stereotype, but to be honest all the Argentine polo players I've met – male and female – were without exception unbelievably glamorous.

There are some polo players in Argentina who clearly lap up this attention, but many others are desperately trying to escape this image of the Argentine polo playboy. 'They've got us wrong,' said Marcial Socas over a glass of Coca-Cola in the kitchen of his Estancia La Martina. 'We're quite normal really, we wear jeans and T-shirts – we're not that jet set.'

True, the Argentine polo player may be marginally less affluent than his British or North American counterpart, and this is because polo is relatively much more financially accessible in Argentina than elsewhere. Still, you do need a certain amount of capital to indulge and therefore it's definitely a sport for Argentina's upper middle classes. 'It's an expensive vice,' polo players joke. In Argentina, a decent polo pony goes for about US$3,000 (the same horse can easily fetch twice or even three times this amount when sold abroad). Of course any self-respecting polo player has at least four horses just to see him through the chukkers. Then there are the saddles, sticks, leather kneepads, helmets, gloves, balls, stable, stable hands, champagne and jet set lifestyle. It all adds up.

Should you decide to play polo, you will also have to devote hours talking shop with fellow polo fanatics. 'All we ever do is talk about horses and polo the whole time,' one player told me, barely dragging his eyes off the game we were watching together from the sidelines. 'You decide if that's passionate or not.'

Polo Etiquette

If you visit a polo club or even an *estancia* while you are living in Argentina someone might well sidle up to you and ask, 'Do you stick and ball?' In polo lingo, this means 'Do you know how to play polo?' (They'll probably ask you this in English as, among their many attributes, polo players also tend to be bilingual.) Answer 'yes' only if you're fairly good at polo. Argentine polo is played incredibly fast and the players are completely fearless. 'If you fall off your horse in England, they'll probably call an ambulance,' said Charlie, who spent a year polishing up his polo skills on an *estancia* outside Buenos Aires. 'But here they are like, 'What are you doing down there on the ground? *Vamos*!' So unless, of course, you do 'stick and ball', you'll probably be much better off watching the game from the sidelines.

As a polo spectator, it's easy to get confused. Put simply, two teams of four players try to hit a small wooden or plastic ball through two large goals at opposite ends of an enormous field. They are mounted on horses – polo ponies aren't ponies but fully grown horses – and armed with wooden mallets, which they whirl ferociously through the air as they gallop across the pitch like wild dervishes. It all makes for a rather terrifying and invigorating spectacle.

All this lasts for seven frantic minutes, or a 'chukker'. After each chukker, the players race off the pitch, leap onto fresh mounts and start all over again. Matches last for between six and eight chukkers, depending on the standard of the players.

As you'd imagine, polo involves a fair amount of unpleasant accidents and broken collarbones, even though practically all the rules are concerned with safety. A good polo player requires a certain devil-may-care attitude that must be rather appealing to the glamorous girlfriends on the sidelines.

HITTING THE SLOPES

For many people, mountains mean skiing and in August thousands of Argentines with the means to indulge head for the slopes of the Andes. During this time of year the weather reports are avidly watched and the season's first heavy snowfall makes headline news across the country. If the snow reports look good you pack up and leave. Argentina's main ski resorts are Bariloche, Las Leñas, Chapelco (near San Martín de Los Andes) and the more isolated Ushuaia in Tierra del Fuego. Snow shortages and high winds can be a hindrance.

'In Argentina you don't just say, let's go skiing this winter, you say, *if there's snow*, let's go skiing this winter,' says Nico Busch, a member of the Argentine Ski Club.

What's more, Argentines don't go to these resorts just to ski; they go to have fun. There is probably not such a fantastic level of skiing as you might see in Europe. If the weather's bad, they wouldn't dream of stoically going out and braving it. They'd much rather stay in and drink hot chocolate, saving up their energy for a night of partying. Likewise, if it's been a heavy night on the tiles, you stay in bed until your hangover's worn off. 'I don't know of any other place in the world where skiers consistently go to bed at 6:00 am and get up in the afternoon,' says Nico.

MUSIC AND SONG CONTESTS

Argentines have an unbelievably high tolerance level for noise and generally there is always music blaring out from somewhere. Argentine rock is famous throughout Latin America, although it is still to take the foreign markets by storm. And even though I've never before been to a country with such an obsession with the Rolling Stones, Argentina has produced its own fair share of contemporary rock legends. Charly Garcia – his naturally two-toned black-and-white moustache is one of the world's greatest mysteries – and Fito Paez effortlessly fill stadiums and sing songs that reflect the reality of Argentine life. They have a rebellious streak – Garcia's rendition of the Argentine national anthem once landed him in court.

At the other end of the spectrum are the folkloric singers Mercedes Sosa and the younger up-and-coming Soledad Pastorutti, who was a teenager when she released her first album. Both are hugely popular among Argentina's youth, proving that *folklorico* isn't just for fuddy-duddies. In fact, Sosa frequently appears with Garcia on stage.

You won't have to head to packed stadiums to hear Argentine music at its best. Spontaneous song contests (*payadas*) take place in crowded unpretentious bars. Competitors are often dressed in the full gaucho get-up – baggy *bombacha* trousers, sombrero, *rastra* and neck scarf, complete with a large curling *facón* stuck into their waistband. These men leap up and improvise verses, challenging the other troubadours in the room, who in turn sing a withering response between puffs on their cigarettes and swigs of red wine. Stumbling into a bar in the Buenos Aires suburb of Mataderos one late Sunday afternoon, we found an entire room entranced by these *payadores*, heads swivelling from one end to the other like spectators at a tennis match. All the time, the barman, who doubled up as the guitarist, never missed a beat or a chance to refill an empty glass. An especially good verse would be greeted with applause and bravos, begging a response. Anyone who could hold a tune and sing loudly enough was welcome to join in.

THE TANGO

The tango is to Argentina what the *hula* is to Hawaii. It is quintessentially Argentine and this is no mean feat in a country that complains it has few truly national inventions. Tango, of course, is not the only music and dance native to Argentina, but it is by far the most sensational.

Funnily enough, in this most macho of countries, the tango began in a remarkably un-macho way. It was danced by pairs of men as they queued in brothels, to the music of the violin, guitar and flute. Later, the bandoneon was added. This musical instrument – a German invention that looks like a sort of elongated accordion with buttons instead of keys – provides the telltale melancholic wheeze that we associate with the tango today. As the flutes disappeared and a piano was added, the tango seemed to take on a desperately sad air and one that complemented the life of the lonely immigrants who arrived in Buenos Aires at the turn of the century. Enrique Santos Discépolo, a great tango composer, once defined the tango as a 'sad thought that is danced.' A slightly more optimistic critic called it 'the happiness of being sad'.

Underneath its melancholic veneer, the tango can be surprisingly raunchy. 'Dancing the tango is like having an affair that lasts for three minutes,' said a friend who had been seduced by the tango when she arrived in Buenos Aires and avidly taking evening lessons ever since. I could see her point. When you watch a couple dancing the tango, lips a matter of millimetres away on the verge of a kiss and chests pressed close together, it's impossible to believe that they're not having a love affair in real life. The chances are, however, that they're not. In fact, they may never have even spoken to each other before.

A nod, a smile or a glance to the dance floor is enough for a man to invite a woman to dance the tango. He then walks over to her table and she stands up to meet him. No words are exchanged. *Never*, in Argentina, will a woman be so bold as to invite a man to dance the tango. This sounds terribly macho, but it is an unbreakable rule that is adhered to at all costs. Once on the floor, it is the man again who leads. He moves forward, she moves backward. The subtle pressure of his hand on her back lets her know a change of direction or when to perform a gliding figure of eight step known as an *ocho*. They also both need an inbuilt radar to avoid colliding with other couples on the dance floor – technically a big tango no-no.

Tango fashion has a distinct look that tells of its origins in city brothels. Fishnet stockings, high heels and clingy dresses are *de rigueur* for women, lacquered hair and neck-scarves for men. Preferred colours are red and black. Mind you, while some tango dancers look like they've just stepped out of a cabaret, with gloves up to their elbows and feathers in their hair, others may well appear in jeans and a T-shirt. Still, no female tango dancer worth her salt would even dream of dancing in anything lower that two-inch heels! In fact, tango lyrics frequently refer to clothes: *Don't you remember that with me you wore your first hat and some leather belt that I stole/ Didn't I bring you, for your saint's day, a lovely pair of earrings that I nicked from that jerk's room one night/ As well as those suede boots and that great silk skirt ...*

But above all, tango touches upon matters of the heart, or rather the broken heart. The song that Argentines generally consider one of the greatest tangos ever released tells the story of a man, probably a pimp, complaining bitterly about the loss of his lover. *Mi Noche Triste* (My Sad Night) was the first tango sung in public by Carlos Gardel. This is a rough translation of Pascual Contursi's lyrics:

> *Woman, you left me during the most important period of my life*
> *You are leaving me with a broken soul and thorns in my heart*
> *You knew that I really loved you*
> *And that you were the source of my joy and my torrid dreams*
> *I am now without consolation and am getting drunk to help me*
> *   forget.*

Teen angst has nothing on this.

The Magic of Gardel

Carlos Gardel was born in Toulouse, France in 1890, and taken to Buenos Aires at the age of 3 years by his single mother. Some historians have suggested that he might have been Uruguayan, and there's even doubt that his real name was Gardel. But whatever his origins, there's no doubt that once Carlos Gardel opened his mouth he was 100 per cent *porteño*. It is his face with the perennial smile beneath the trilby that beams from photos in old cafés throughout the country.

In 1917, Gardel did what no *porteño* had ever done before; he sang a tango – *Mi Noche Triste* – in front of a genteel *porteño* audience at the Esmeralda Theatre in Buenos Aires. Tangos had been sung before, but only in bars and houses of disrepute. Now suddenly here was a man singing about a brokenhearted pimp that had decided to get drunk. What's more, he was singing in *lunfardo*, the local street slang of Buenos Aires. It was a tremendous hit!

Sadly, Carlos Gardel was killed in a plane crash in Colombia in 1935, cutting short a promising film career. Dozens of fans were so

A fan of Gardel croons tangos in San Telmo's Sunday antiques market.

distraught that they tried to commit suicide. More than 60 years after his death, Argentines talk about Gardel as though he's still alive. A common Argentine saying claims that 'Gardel sings better every day'. If someone's singing is not up to scratch, a real put-down would be, 'He's no Gardel.' (*Ouch!*) And when Diego Maradona scored a third goal against Greece in the 1994 World Cup, a popular Argentine radio journalist, beside himself with excitement, whooped, 'Gardel is alive! Gardel is alive!'

How to Become a Tanguero

There are two ways to enjoy tango in Argentina – as an observer and as an active participant. For the former, there is no end of venues where you can watch glitzy professionals perform electrifying tangos while enjoying a drink or an evening meal. And even if this seems slightly touristy, you won't be disappointed.

103

These polished shows probably aren't what you'd imagine tango to be all about. Where are the smoky bars, the glamorous clientele, the Carlos Gardels? For the real thing, you must go to a *milonga* (a tango hall). Here, for just a few pesos, you can walk in and drink, dance tango or just observe the absolute novelty of your surroundings. Every night, hundreds of true tango aficionados congregate in these *milongas*, silently and deftly gliding around the dance floor with the grace of 1930s movie stars. Old-timers, known as *tangueros*, dressed in neck-scarves and impeccable suits, invite high-heeled partners onto the floor, or sit round tables smoking and drinking red wine while eyeing up potential dance partners. You will feel you've walked into some sort of time warp.

At first sight this might look fairly intimidating, but don't let that put you off. A surprising number of younger Argentines are now taking up the tango too. Still, if you're a complete novice, you should go to a *milonga* that holds tango lessons earlier in the evening before a dance. That way, when someone nods in your direction, you can get up and not make a complete fool of yourself.

My first tango lesson was spent dancing lovingly with, well, a chair. But by lesson number two I had found a dance partner. His name was Nicolas, a 22-year-old graphic designer from Buenos Aires with extremely long hair and flared jeans. I was surprised. This was not the stereotypical *tanguero* I'd been expecting.

'It's all the rage among our age group now,' he told me. 'I guess it's fashionable in Europe so that makes it fashionable here.'

'There's a tango revival going on in the whole world,' Mario Sejas, the administrative director of Argentina's National Tango Academy, told me. 'Now it's beginning to capture the young as well. Old people like myself lived in a time when tango was the only music that we could listen to. This was lost by later generations and they stopped playing it altogether on the radio, but for the last few years it has been making a comeback. You can now hear it at more places and you can dance it in more places.' Argentina now boasts a cable channel, *Solo Tango*, a radio station at 92.7 FM that belts out 24-hour nonstop tangos, and even three tango magazines, distributed free.

After just two classes, tango certainly got a grip on me and I was raring to go again.

'You see, that's the problem with tango,' Katya, an English friend living in Buenos Aires, confided. 'It's an addiction. First you go once a week, then twice a week, then before you know it you're going every night. I won't even leave the house without my tango shoes now.'

LA FIESTA

The melancholic strains of the tango are counteracted by the boisterous days of Carnival. Held over several days in February, Argentina's Carnival is neither as disorderly as Bolivia's nor as flamboyant and dressy as Brazil's, but it is a time when everyone gets to let their hair down and behave like giddy schoolboys. Two key ingredients put the oomph! into Argentina's carnival: water bombs and cans of fake snow. You should know in advance that these will be chucked at you and sprayed onto you at any given moment. Everyone is considered fair game. Other festivals – especially those in the northwest of the country – can be equally boisterous with packed plazas, gaucho parades and *asados* (barbecues) sizzling on every corner.

Calendar of Festivals and Public Holidays

Practically every day in the year is claimed by some commemoration, be it Mother's Day, Father's Day, Lover's Day or just National Dog Day (June 2). Most of these don't amount to more than a fleeting mention in the newspapers and an excuse for a day off work for whoever's special day it is.

The dates that follow are only approximate guidelines, as they tend to change to suit long weekends, the weather, a last-minute whim or a case of *mañanaitis*. To get exact dates closer to the time as well as information on local fiestas, contact the government tourist office whose address is listed in the Strategic Directory, Chapter 10.

Preparing for a gaucho parade in Salta.

January

During the first 15 days, the *Fiesta de Doma y Folklorico* takes place in an amphitheatre in Jesus Maria, Córdoba. There is a 10-day event with singing, gaucho parades and a spectacular rodeo.

During the last week of January, the National Folkloric Festival is held in Cosquin, Córdoba.

February

Carnival celebrations throughout the country, lasting for two weeks. Particularly spectacular in the northern provinces.

March

During the first week of March, the Vendimia wine festival is held in Mendoza. The central hub is in the open-air amphitheatre in

Mendoza's Parque San Martín. Grapes are stamped by beauty queens, and there is music and dancing. Book early for accommodation.

March/April, Easter week celebrations throughout the country. National holidays on Maundy Thursday, Good Friday and Easter Day.

May

1, Labour Day, national holiday.

25, Anniversary of the 1810 revolution, national holiday.

June

10, Brits, keep a low profile: today is Malvinas Day, national holiday.

20, Flag Day (*Día de la Bandera*), another national holiday.

14–20, Salta Week, to commemorate the death of General Martín Guemes with parades, dances and bonfires in Salta.

July

9, Independence Day, national holiday.

August

15, Argentina's only bullfight – *Toreo de la Vincha* – to celebrate the Assumption of the Virgin takes place in Casabindo (Jujuy). The bull, who represents the devil, isn't killed; instead men try to remove ribbons and silver coins from its horns.

17, Anniversary of the death of General José de San Martín, national holiday.

23–24, *Exodo Jujeño*: week-long festivities in Jujuy to celebrate the city's evacuation under General Belgrano's orders in the early 19th century.

September

15, the city of Salta holds a religious festival when images of the Lord and Virgin are paraded through town to prevent earthquakes.

107

October

12, Columbus Day (*Día de la Raza*), national holiday.

Starting the second week of October and lasting 11 days is the *Fiesta del Sol* in San Juan city with folkloric shows, music and exhibitions.

First half of October, Oktoberfest beer festival in the Germanic town of Villa General Belgrano, Córdoba province.

November

1–2, All Souls Day or Day of the Dead celebrated by towns in the Quebrada de Humahuaca (Jujuy).

10, *Día de la Tradicion*. Gaucho festivals are held throughout the country with traditional parades, games, events on horseback, music and dancing. Excellent in San Antonio de Areco, Buenos Aires province.

December

8, Feast of the Immaculate Conception, a non-working optional holiday.

25, Christmas Day, national holiday.

— *Chapter Five* —

BUSINESS CUSTOMS

'He had a lot of stocks and shares
And half a street in Buenos Aires
A bank in Rio, and a line
Of steamers to the Argentine ...'

—Hilaire Belloc, from the poem 'About John'
in the collection *Cautionary Verses*

THE BUSINESS ENVIRONMENT

Looking on the bright side, conducting business in Argentina combines the best of both worlds. Rather like its people, Argentine business involves a wonderful mix of European efficiency and Latin American flexibility. But this is no Latin backwater. The chances are that you'll find yourself dealing with very sophisticated businessmen and women, many of whom hold MBAs from leading universities.

Argentines have a long and strong history of dealing with foreign business. And since the privatisation programmes of the 1990s, when the government sold off most of its bloated and largely defunct state-owned companies into private hands, the rise in foreign investment has been nothing short of meteoric. Foreign investment is actively encouraged and foreign investors now have the same rights and duties as nationals with few restrictions. Import duties and export with-holdings have been reduced and inflation, which broke world records during the late 1980s, is now under control. The Argentine government is also seeking growth through stricter tax and monetary discipline, restoring the market economy and full integration with international markets. Argentina is one of the four members of Mercosur, the Southern Cone Common Market established in 1995 with Brazil, Paraguay and Uruguay which aims to eliminate internal tariffs and can boast a combined population of 200 million.

As a foreigner doing business in Argentina, you will be welcomed with open arms and treated with great friendliness. But don't get too blasé. You should also keep your eyes and ears open, and get everything down on paper and checked by a lawyer. 'Do business as you would in New York or London,' advises Joe Oppenheimer, a German-Brazilian economist who has been working in Argentina since 1970. 'The rules are the same.'

Doing business in Argentina can be a very social affair so the previous chapter on Social Customs should also be consulted.

IT'S NOT WHAT BUT WHO YOU KNOW

As in all Latin American countries, a tremendous amount of networking goes on in Argentina. If you need something done, someone you know will have a cousin who has a friend who is married to someone who can do what you want. It may be a convoluted path but it is often the most effective. Contacts are crucial, and if you plan to do business with or in Argentina make it a priority to develop as large a network of contacts as possible. To phone someone up and say 'I was given your name by so and so' will be a hundred times more effective than a cold call. This sort of name-dropping is rampant within the Argentine community, so don't think twice about joining in yourself. Any previous Argentine business partners, friends, even relations if you can dig some up, are ideal starting points. If you really are arriving completely cold, your local chamber of commerce or embassy should be able to point you in the right direction.

Once initial contacts have been made, make the time and effort to build lasting personal ties. These will always pay off in the end. You should never walk away from an Argentine associate on bad terms, even if you don't want to cut a deal. Argentine business is a very personalised world and if you leave on a bad note word might get around, closing doors to you later on.

You should also bear in mind that nepotism is perfectly acceptable in Argentina's business environment; in many cases, it is even expected. In some companies jobs and deals will be given to family members and close friends of the family first. This is especially the case in smaller companies, family-run businesses and in the government. In such cases, you can name-drop to your heart's content, but you will still come in second.

FORGING BUSINESS RELATIONSHIPS

The better your relationship with your Argentine colleagues, the better your chances are of doing good business and reaching a deal. Luckily, Argentines are more than happy to be wooed. In the process of forging good relations, you will be required to put in a lot of preparatory hard work, tucking into long lunches and getting stuck in conversations on every subject except the business at hand. By the time you've wined and dined with your Argentine business associates, as is customary, you should be left with rewarding friendships as well as contracts. 'It's like a courtship,' says Oppenheimer. 'You need a lot of subtlety. Try not to show that you want the deal that badly, you're going to have to beat about the bush a little.'

It is also important to note that many Argentines often value the person with whom they do business more than the name of the company. If you change your negotiating team halfway through, you may undermine previous good relations or even an entire contract.

Greetings and Meetings

Argentines are very warm and effusive. Friends and acquaintances greet each other with hugs and kisses. Even at a business meeting, unless it is very formal, introductions may be accompanied by kisses. Women kiss women, men kiss women, but men will shake hands with other men at the first meeting, especially in a business setting. If men know each other well, they will also kiss each other on the cheek. This may sound shockingly un-macho, but it is very telling of their Italian origins. Just across the border, in Chile or Brazil for example, men wouldn't dream of kissing each other hello.

It is unlikely that you'll plunge straight into the business at hand as soon as you walk through the door. After the effusive greetings, conversation will probably move on to social chitchat. Brush up on topics such as football, and be prepared to answer questions on your family, as these will almost certainly crop up. Keep the conversation light. Sensitive subjects such as the Dirty War, the Malvinas-Falkland islands, relations with Chile, military dictatorships and government corruption can still touch a raw nerve and are best avoided in a business setting. Only when all the pleasantries have been dispensed with can you get down to business.

Once the meeting is over, don't run off straight away; it would be taken as an insult. Again, social niceties are called for. Allow things to run their natural course and wait until your Argentine hosts make the first move to leave.

Gift Giving

The question of whether or not to give presents is a grey area in business around the globe, and Argentina is no exception. Argentine companies have not arrived at the stage where gift giving is deemed inappropriate, but you still want to make it clear that your gift is just that, and not a bribe.

If your Argentine counterpart has young children you could bring a small gift for them – perhaps a football or rugby shirt from your home country. Gifts like these are always appreciated and can't possibly be misconstrued. Flowers are also welcome, especially if you are invited to the home of your business partners (in which case you should never arrive empty-handed). You could bring along a present that is connected with your business or your country's culture: a glossy coffee-table book, for example, or if you represent a winery, a bottle or two of your own wine. Women, however, should exercise a little more caution when giving gifts to male colleagues in case it is misconstrued as a personal overture.

Christmas is a traditional – and suitable – time for gift giving in the Argentine business world.

The Art of Greasing Palms

Argentine law makes a difference between *propinas* (tips or incentive payments), which are legal and help speed things up that are going to be done anyway, and *coimas* (bribes), which are illegal. Someone who solicits a bribe is known as a *coimero* and is liable to criminal prosecution, as is the person who gives the bribe. Yet bribing is rife, and as one foreign businessman pointed out, 'there are a lot of bribable people out there'. *Coimeros* may well seek you out, and in some cases this might make things run more smoothly. If confronted with such a situation, you should always use your own judgement but remember that bribery can be a bottomless pit. At best you might get away with having a reputation of being a 'sucker' who always 'pays up'; at worst you could wind up in jail.

Even *propinas* are now becoming less and less common as the conditions that encouraged them are slowly being removed with the privatisation of state companies and larger firms.

LABOUR

Argentina has the most skilled and highest paid labour force in Latin America, with a workforce of over 13 million people. Unfortunately, unemployment and underemployment continue to plague the country. The recent privatisation of state-owned firms, increasing use of labour-saving technologies, trends towards a freer labour market and the overwhelming effect of the 1995 Tequila crisis have all led to rising unemployment, which at the time of writing stands at over 14 per cent. The privatisation of railroads alone cost 110,000 jobs.

Due to the relatively high cost of living in Argentina and faced with an economy in recession, many Argentines now work longer shifts for less pay and – if they can find the work – may hold down two jobs. There is also a vast number of labourers working the black market, who are paid 'cash in hand' for unskilled or low-skilled jobs. Estimates suggest that as many as 30 per cent of Argentina's workforce survive in this way. Their wages are low, their hours long and they receive no benefits. None of them pay any taxes either.

Many of these black-market labourers are from neighbouring South American countries and have entered the country illegally. Recently there has been increasing nationalist backlash against them, with charges that they are taking work away from Argentines. Yet many of these illegal immigrants do the work no one else wants to do for such little pay.

Workers' Rights and Conditions of Employment

The 48-hour work week is standard in Argentina. Workers must have a minimum of 12 hours off between consecutive workdays and those in hazardous occupations are limited by law to a 6-hour day. Saturday afternoons and Sundays are obligatory rest days, although overtime is permitted and those employed in the service sector, particularly, tend to work over weekends. Children under the age of 14 are forbidden from working with certain exceptions for those employed in family-run businesses and in farming. A one and a half hour lunch break is standard in Argentina, although workers under the age of 18 and female employees are entitled to two-hour lunch breaks (with some exemptions).

The minimum wage is US$1 an hour or US$200 a month (most jobs pay substantially more) and a 13th month salary is compulsory, half of which must be paid at the end of June and the remainder at the end of the calendar year. In 1996, the average monthly salary was US$867. The average monthly manufacturing wage is about US$875, while managers and professionals can earn between $1,000 and $5,000 a month and sometimes more. Top executives may earn more than their North American counterparts.

Paid vacations range from 14 to 35 days a year in addition to the 11 national holidays listed in Chapter 4, but workers must be employed for at least six months to qualify. Employees who have worked for less than six months are entitled to one day's paid holiday for every 20 days of work, which works out much the same.

Medical benefits and pension schemes are in force in Argentina, with mandatory contributions of 23 per cent of a worker's wage from the employer and 17 per cent from the employee. Employers must also contribute 9 per cent of their employee's wages towards a family allowance payment for the worker and additional amounts for worker's compensation, unemployment, disability and insurance benefits. Fringe benefits such as subsidised meals, transport and housing are at the employer's discretion.

TRADE UNIONS

Labour unions have traditionally been massive and centralised in Argentina. They peaked under Perón's government in the 1940s and 1950s when at one stage 50 per cent of workers belonged to unions.

Trade union membership is now half that and although labour unions continue to be particularly strong in the metallurgical, automobile and banking industries and among state employees, they are losing some of their once formidable economic and political clout.

Union membership is voluntary and union members have their union dues deducted from their wages and forwarded to the union by their employer.

HIRING AND FIRING

Many jobs in Argentina begin with a three-month trial period – which can renewed up to three times – during which time the employer decides whether to take that person on permanently. During this time, which can last as long as nine months, the employee will receive few benefits (no paid vacation, no pension scheme). He or she can also be dismissed without any severance pay or advance notice of termination. Once this trial period is over, the employee is either hired or dropped. If hired, he or she then has full worker's rights.

Argentina has fairly strict laws on termination of employment. If an employee is fired with no reasonable cause then he or she is entitled to an advance notice of at least one month and severance pay at the rate of one month's salary for each year served with the company. If dismissal is a result of provable lack of work then the indemnity is cut by half. Such strict procedures have been criticised for hindering employment as many employers are afraid to take on the added risks of compensation, preferring instead to use mandatory overtime or black-market labourers.

WOMEN IN THE WORKPLACE

Women in managerial positions are still such a rarity in Argentina that newspapers run articles on this strange breed. But with no more than 10 per cent of management positions being occupied by women, Argentina is still leagues ahead of most other Latin American nations in regard to equal opportunities. Meanwhile, a new generation of highly qualified female graduates is emerging, suggesting further change is on the way and that traditional macho prejudices are going to have to give way sooner or later.

Having said this, you are still dealing with a fairly macho society. Visiting businesswomen will be under as much pressure as their female Argentine counterparts to look glamorous and immaculately turned out. Should you walk down the street, let alone visit a factory, brace yourself for *piropos* (suggestive comments) and sidelong glances from men. You are also bound to be asked about your marital status and whether or not you have any children. Such questions aren't meant to be personal intrusions, but rather highlight Argentines' genuine interest in and love of family life.

Although women form just a small percentage of Argentina's managerial scene, they still hold considerable clout at home. As a visiting businesswoman, you should be aware (and beware) of the possibility of jealous wives and girlfriends of your male Argentine business associates. They could easily cause business relations to collapse. It is not unheard of for female partners and employees to be dropped because of pressure back at home.

Trophy Wives and Secretaries

When President Menem visited England in the autumn of 1998 – the first visit by an Argentine president since the Falklands/Malvinas war – he chose Zulemita, his lithe and glamorous 28-year-old daughter, to accompany him on the trip. The gossip papers had a field day with the very photogenic president's daughter and wickedly suggested that he was hoping to marry her off to Prince Andrew. They were probably wrong. The simple fact is that in Argentina a beautiful woman hanging on your arm gives you a huge amount of kudos and enhances your political or business image no end.

The 'trophy wife' theme extends from the bedroom to the board-room. Generally, the more successful your business, the prettier your secretaries. Argentine men can be maddeningly sexist at times!

THE LANGUAGE BARRIER

Many Argentines speak English, especially those belonging to the business community, but any efforts at speaking Spanish on your part will be very much appreciated.

Don't think you can go it alone, however, when it comes to marketing your product locally. If you imagine that translation will be the least of your worries, think again. Everyone still giggles at the case of General Motors when it tried to market its Chevy Nova in Latin America. In Spanish, *nova* means a type of star but said out loud it might just as well have been *no va*, which means 'it doesn't go'. Needless to say, sales rocketed after the name was changed.

But General Motors' *faux pas* was nothing compared to that of one US chicken chain which decided, when expanding into the Latin American market, to stick with its successful US slogan: 'It takes a tough man to make a tender chicken.' Unfortunately, in the translation, the slogan came across as 'It takes a man with a hard-on to make a chicken affectionate.' Argentines, I'm sure, would have found this hysterical. But I'm equally sure that no macho Argentine worth his salt would have bought that chicken.

Language mix-ups such as these can work both ways. One Argentine restaurant, in an attempt to attract English-speaking customers, translated its menu into English. Unfortunately, it appeared to be offering 'revolting eggs' for breakfast and 'smashed potatoes' for lunch. An interesting combination to say the least!

Translation and Interpreter Services

Good interpreters come at a price – about US$330 for half a day's work. There are cheaper options, but you generally get what you pay for. Even so, it is advisable to check costs before contracting an interpreter; some may count a short meeting as half a day's work and charge you accordingly.

Your embassy should be able to provide you with a list of known interpreters and authorised translators. Hotels may also be able to help and it's always a good idea to check the classified section in the English language daily, the *Buenos Aires Herald.*

Note that business documents must be translated into Spanish by authorised public translators to have any legal standing in Argentina.

TIMEKEEPING AND OFFICE HOURS

If you are an obsessive timekeeper, you might as well bang your head against a brick wall in Argentina. It may at times look like Europe, smell like Europe and even talk like Europe, but Argentina is Latin America and runs on Latin time frames, unless of course English timing – *hora inglesa* or *hora americana* – is specified. Having said that, punctuality on your part for business meetings is important, even if your hosts don't show up on time themselves. You can gauge the importance of a particular meeting to your Argentine colleagues by their punctuality: a very important meeting will probably start on time. Argentines accustomed to doing international business are generally much more punctual than the rest of the country.

In Argentina, the *mañana* syndrome, or procrastination, isn't as bad as it is in many other Latin American countries, but it does exist to a certain degree. If someone tries to brush you off until tomorrow (*mañana*), get tough. Let them know you're only in the country for a few days (even if this is not strictly true) and that you have to be seen today *or else*. Still, you should expect things to take longer in Argentina and thus budget your time accordingly. You should also be prepared to invest considerable time in forging successful business relations. The worst thing you could do is come to Argentina with an attitude of 'let's get this over and done with as soon as possible'. Not only would such an approach be considered inappropriate business etiquette, it is also completely impractical in Argentina.

Generally, business hours begin between 8:00 and 10:00 am and end between 5:30 and 7:00 pm, Monday through Friday. Top executives tend to arrive after their secretaries, at around 10:00 am and stay on later in the evening.

Photo: Jamie Grant

Soaking up the last of the summer sun, businessmen in Buenos Aires take a well-earned lunch break.

Government offices are open from 12:30 pm to 7:30 pm in winter, and from 7:30 am to 1:00 pm in summer. Banks are generally open between 10:00 am and 3:00 pm Monday to Friday. (*Note:* Banks are closed on all the national holidays listed in Chapter 4, and also on December 30 and on Bank Employee Day, November 6.)

In the countryside, the institution of the siesta is alive and well, and many businesses may close between 2:00 pm and 5:00 pm. But as business becomes more international this custom, sadly, is becoming less acceptable. In Buenos Aires, where a siesta would probably do everyone some good, it is now practically unheard of. Even the traditional long lunches accompanied by a bottle or two of wine are no longer everyday occurrences. Lunch may be just a sandwich grabbed between meetings.

The Argentines are night owls at heart so don't be horrified if your Argentine counterpart decides to schedule a meeting as late as 8:00 pm. Breakfast meetings, on the other hand, are practically unheard of, not least owing to the fact that breakfast is not considered a serious meal in Argentina; typical early morning traffic chaos is another obstacle. If you are calling the shots or running on a tight schedule, you might, however, be able to get away with insisting on a business breakfast, but lunch is undoubtedly the best bet if you want to do business over the dining table.

Finally, don't even think about trying to do business during the holiday season. Offices are deserted during January and February (summer holidays) and for the middle two weeks of July (winter vacation). If there has been a good snowfall in the Andes, you shouldn't be surprised if your Argentine colleagues nip off at the last minute for a few days' skiing as well.

(*Note:* The 24-hour clock is widely used in Argentina. This is probably due to the fact that 1:00 in the morning is often just as pulsating as 1:00 in the afternoon.)

BUSINESS ATTIRE

Argentines can be terribly fashion-conscious and are bound to judge you, at least initially, on your appearance. Think more 'London' – subtle and understated – than anything too flowery or straight off the latest catwalks of Europe. Conservative dark suits for both sexes really can't go wrong, 'Although a great Italian suit,' a foreign businessman confided, 'will work wonders in Buenos Aires.'

During the summer months (December to March) businessmen usually wear lightweight suits and businesswomen wear lightweight cotton or linen dresses and trousers. In winter (June to August) woollen clothing, overcoats and an umbrella will be necessary.

If business extends to evening entertainment, you may be expected to change into something dressier. Gala nights at the opera or ballet usually mean black tie or evening dress. Also be prepared for the fact that some restaurants, clubs and casinos have a strict dress code. (Also see 'What to Wear', page 220.)

WORK AND BUSINESS VISAS

Those wishing to work in Argentina must obtain a work visa from the Argentine consulate in their home country before travelling to Argentina. The Argentine company that plans to employ you is required to apply for the visa on your behalf in Argentina. There is a charge of about $330. Work visas – which last for between one and three years – can also be obtained within Argentina from the *Dirección Nacional de Migraciones* but it is a long-drawn-out bureaucratic process that can last several months, and you may even be required to leave the country until the visa is secured.

Visitors on business are also technically required to have a business visa prior to travel to Argentina, but most visitors – if they are in the country for less than 90 days – enter on a tourist visa to minimise paperwork.

TAXES

Buenos Aires itself originally flourished thanks to illegal smuggling and skilfully getting around Spain's colonial trade laws, and the legacy of tax evasion has survived to this day. Tax evasion, it is frequently joked, is a national sport in Argentina!

Needless to say, Argentina's tax authorities have long suspected that much is escaping them. They have tried to make collection procedures more efficient and close loopholes in the system, while simultaneously introducing heavy fines and even imprisonment for noncompliance. Still, they estimate that one-third of taxes due are not being paid. Tax dodgers argue that this high degree of tax evasion is justified by the high degree of government corruption.

As a foreigner conducting business in Argentina, don't even think about dodging your taxes. The bottom line is to comply with all the laws and regulations.

The finer ramifications of the Argentine tax system may be ambiguous and confusing, so it is a good idea to employ local specialists to guide you. At the time of writing, residents and resident corporations (those incorporated in Argentina) are taxed on worldwide income. Nonresidents and nonresident corporations are taxed only on Argentine-source income. Corporate tax is payable at the rate of 33 per cent. Income tax rates for Argentine residents range from 6 per cent to 33 per cent; for nonresidents it is a flat rate of 33 per cent.

The federal government also imposes a capital gains tax, a value added tax (VAT – IVA in Spanish) on most goods at 21 per cent, a tax on assets, an excise tax and customs duties. Provincial governments are responsible for levying turnover tax, real estate tax, stamp tax, tax on vehicles and tax on public entertainment, among others.

Paying Taxes

If you work for an Argentine company, your employer is obliged to register you with the tax authority, file tax returns and retain taxes from your salary. If you are self-employed or earn an additional non-wage income, you must declare yourself at the tax office – *Dirección General Impositiva* (DGI). Tax returns for individuals are filed annually in June, when you declare your earnings for the previous calendar year.

Corporations are required to make 11 monthly advance payments, each at 8.5 per cent of the previous year's tax. The corporate tax return must be filed within five months after the end of the corporation's fiscal year.

MORE BUSINESS TIPS
• When dealing with numbers, full stops punctuate thousands and commas indicate decimal points.

- Don't schedule back-to-back meetings, as you could run into the most awful domino effect and end up being late for everything.
- Give a firm handshake; this is a sign of both strength (machismo at work again) and sincerity (you can trust me).
- Argentines tend to communicate in close proximity. Don't back away.
- A large quantity of business cards to distribute will prove invaluable and help clarify your status.
- Try not to get flustered about smoking. It's still a perfectly acceptable custom in Argentina where nearly every man and his dog puffs away. If you do light up, it is polite to offer your cigarettes around to others in the room.
- Just as you may have called upon a contact, you will be expected to reciprocate and use your own contacts to help out when called upon yourself.
- Try to get people's direct telephone numbers, or your call may get lost in a maze of secretaries, departments and ghastly electronic music.
- If you're not sure what to wear, err on the side of formality. A book should not be judged by its cover, but – initially at least – you will be.
- Any invitations, business or social, made in a social context should be reconfirmed later. Argentines aim to please and may accept an invitation that they have no intention of keeping.

Doing business in Argentina teaches you the capacity to react fast to a changing and unpredictable environment. It will be very challenging and never boring and will make you use all your skills, intelligence and intuition. If you're the sort of person who likes a stable, repetitive business environment, then Argentina is probably not the country for you.

Business contacts are listed in the Strategic Directory, Chapter 10.

— Chapter Six —

FOOD AND DRINK

'Their manners at table are ultra Bohemian. They read the papers, shout vehemently at each other, sprawl their limbs under and over the table, half swallow their knives, spit with true Yankee freedom on the carpeted floor, gesticulate and bend across the table in the heat of an argument, smoke cigarettes between the courses, and even while a course of which some of them do no partake is serving …'

—19th century visitor Thomas Turner
on Argentine table manners

Eating in Argentina is no mere routine. It is an event, a fabulous social affair and the perfect excuse for what Argentines do best – socialising. Needless to say, Argentines are enormously arrogant about both their food and their cooking prowess. Beef, however, is the *pièce de résistance*. That their beef is the best in the world is a fact that will be stated to you frequently and quite categorically.

To crown it all, Argentines seem to have an inborn talent that enables them to cook their *bife* to perfection. Newly arrived in Argentina, I watched a *porteño* friend prepare a steak. With a lethally sharpened knife he sliced through the raw flesh like butter, casually dropped it into a frying pan, dextrously browned both sides with a skilful flip of his wrist and then set it down on the table in front of me – unashamedly bragging that it would be the best steak I would ever eat. Infuriatingly, it was.

WHAT'S ON THE MENU

Argentina's menu reflects its migrant population. For a country that became rich on cattle, it's hardly surprising that beef dominates the menu. But the Italian influence can easily be seen in the abundant choice of pizza, pasta and delectable ice cream. Any standard restaurant menu will include an enormous variety of raviolis, cannellonis, spaghettis and lasagnas as well as steaks the size of small houses, all served with *papas fritas* (french fries) and crunchy salads. (Argentines don't go in for green vegetables in a big way.)

Along with the Italians, other immigrants have introduced such delights as Welsh cream teas in Chubut, kosher meals in Buenos Aires and Alpine chocolate in Córdoba. In the northwest, where the Andean culture is still strong, regional dishes such as *carbonada* – a meat stew – and mouthwatering *empanadas* (meat or cheese patties) are widely available. In short, you are unlikely to get bored or go hungry unless, of course, you're a strict vegetarian. Vegetarians get the short straw in Argentina. As a veggie, you'll be chastised and told that you're missing the best of Argentina. I've even known vegetarian friends who have been fed meat in disguise by baffled waiters who can't understand why on earth anyone wouldn't want to eat Argentine beef.

THE SACRED COW?

In 1580, Juan de Garay drew up the original city plan of Buenos Aires on a piece of cowhide. A popular gaucho game – *taba* – involves throwing a piece of cow bone and betting on which side will face up when it lands. *Carne* in other Spanish-speaking countries means meat in general but in Argentina it means just one thing: beef. In Argentina, beef is big business – to prove it, Argentines eat on average an astonishing 59 kilograms of beef a year each!

Argentines have always been insatiable carnivores thanks to the abundant cattle herds that have roamed the pampas ever since Pedro Mendoza's ill-fated expedition in 1536. Argentine cattle have kept the domestic market well supplied with beef since colonial times and there has always been plenty left over to export abroad. South of the Río Colorado, where the lush grasslands of the pampas turn into the plains of Patagonia, cattle are swapped for sheep, and in the kitchen, lamb largely replaces beef.

Given such enormous quantities of meat, at only a fraction of the price it would cost in other countries, Argentines cook it in the most sensible way – hurling it onto grills over hot coals and open fires in the greatest of all Argentine institutions – the *asado*.

The Ultimate Beef Fest

The *asado* is a wildly popular Argentine barbecue, which involves the consumption of enormous quantities of meat, sloshed down with gallons of red wine in the company of friends and family. Practically every house with a garden or patio will have a *parrilla* (the grill for making the *asado*) and every Argentine knows how to throw a wonderful *asado* party. The rules are simple: the men cook the meat and the women make the salad. It's a macho rule but one that everyone seems perfectly happy with. It is a matter of pride to the Argentine male that he gets his *asado* going without any help or suggestions from others, particularly – heaven forbid! – a woman. I once observed a man in Salta surreptitiously resorting to his girlfriend's hairdryer to keep the flame alight.

Those unfortunate enough to have to work on the weekends – the classic *asado* time – won't go without their meat fix either. Even in urban centres, impromptu sizzling barbecues are set up on the roadside next to potholes and pneumatic drills, or in the middle of dusty building sites. Hard hats momentarily cast aside, everyone congregates around the *parrilla* and tucks into the usual vast quantities of meat.

Instead of attending an outdoor barbecue, Argentines may flock to a *parrilla*, an Argentine steakhouse. Here, the meat is still cooked over open coals, but this time by an *asador*. The *asador* is something of a local hero. He is normally a bear of a man who swelters over the *parrilla*, stoking the coals with one hand and battering out hunks of beef and entrails with the other. It is he we must thank for cooking the meat to perfection.

The main cuts of beef are *bife de chorizo* (a thick juicy rump steak cut off the rib), *bife de lomo* (sirloin), *bife de costilla* (T-bone steak), *tira de asado* (strip of rib) and *vacio* (a flavoursome cut similar to sirloin). Don't miss out on the *matambre* either. This is a flank steak stuffed with boiled eggs and vegetables, rolled up and usually served cold. If you like your beef rare, ask for it *jugoso*; if you want it well done then ask for *bien hecho*; medium-cooked is *a punto*. Served alongside these enormous steaks are even more meaty titbits.

Practically every bit of the cow is eaten in Argentina, including all its innards and entrails, tongue and tail. Argentines, however, draw the line at lungs. Assorted offaly accompaniments include *chinchulines* (small intestines), also known affectionately as *chinchis*, which are served with lemon and surprisingly popular among women; *tripa gorda* (large intestines); *ubre* (udder) – they say it tastes milky; *riñones* (kidneys); *corazon* (heart); *higado* (liver); *mollejas* (sweet-

Photo: Jamie Grant

El Asador *stands proud in front of a very carnivorous feast.*

breads); *lengua* (tongue) – best cooked in vinegar; *sesos* (brain); *chorizo* (spicy pork sausage); and *morcilla* (rich blood sausage), which tastes wonderful pasted onto bread as an appetiser.

If you order the *parrillada*, you will get all of these piled on a sizzling hot plate brought to your table along with juicy cuts of beef (and chicken and lamb, if you so wish). And don't miss out on a hunk of *provoletta*, a delectable golden cheese melted and sizzled over the *parrilla*. Unless you're extraordinarily hungry, don't even think about tackling one of these on your own. Bring some friends, preferably a rugby team, along with you.

Also worth a mention is a spicy hot sauce made with herbs, oil and vinegar called *chimichurri*. Its name is rumoured to have come from English immigrants demanding 'give me curry'. *Chimichurri* won't burn the roof of your mouth off, and in a world of steak and salad it adds a welcome spicy punch.

129

SOMETHING FISHY?

If you think that Argentina's 5,000 kilometres of coastline should throw up all sorts of tasty seafood dishes, you're in for a shock. Although Argentina is a big fish producer and exporter, Argentines on the whole are not big fish eaters. There are, however, a few fishy surprises in store that shouldn't be missed if they come your way. The first is centolla, a spectacular king crab and a speciality from Tierra del Fuego, where it is scooped out of the Beagle Channel. It is also eagerly gobbled up by the neighbouring Chileans – big seafood eaters. Also keep your eyes open for pejerrey, a great fish from inland rivers and lakes, as well as the dorado and the monstrous surubi catfish – both caught in the rivers of the northeast.

When eating or ordering seafood always take local advice. The red tide (*marea roja*) periodically affects shellfish in the area with deadly results.

... AND SOMETHING SWEET

Argentines have a notoriously sweet tooth, so it was obvious that they would invent *dulce de leche* sooner or later. This sticky, decadent concoction of caramelised milk is an Argentine classic and can be bought in tubs from supermarkets and corner shops throughout the country. It is a standard spread for bread, croissants and cakes and is used in much the same way that the rest of us use jam or marmalade. There is also *dulce de leche* flavoured ice cream, *dulce de leche* flavoured yogurt and custard cream topped with *dulce de leche*. When Argentines travel abroad, *dulce de leche* is often one of the things they miss most – along with beef, tango and *mate*.

Obviously *dulce de leche* creations have a monopoly on the dessert menus, but other popular desserts are custard cream (*flan*), fruit salad (*ensalada de fruta*), ice cream (*helado*) and the very Argentine *queso con dulce*, which is a gooey cheese served with quince jam (*dulce de membrillo*) or with sweet potato jam (*dulce de batata*).

DINING OUT

When they are not crowded around their kitchen table like members of a large Sicilian family – incessant chatter over forkfuls of spaghetti flying this way and that – or tucking into a wonderful *asado* in their garden, Argentines love to eat out. Even in times of economic straits everybody eats out as often as they possibly can, if it's only a trip to the local pizzeria on the corner.

Cities and towns are geared towards a restaurant and café culture. Strolling around any plaza or down a main street, the visitor can spot, through café windows, thousands of shiny forks diving into bowls of pasta, slices of pizza held aloft, glistening ice creams, crumbling croissants and gooey pastries being licked off sticky fingers.

Eating Hours

Dinner is probably the main meal of the day, with lunch coming a close second. Sometimes this is reversed: big lunch, small dinner. Mind you, Argentines are quite capable of sitting down to a hearty meal at both, accompanied by litres of the local wine and finished off with powerful espressos. Breakfast, on the other hand, is a non-event. At its most extravagant, it is a standard fare of *media lunas* (croissants) and coffee, but more often than not it is just a *café con leche* (a large milky coffee) or a shared *mate*. They have, you must remember, probably just stepped off the dance floor and a light breakfast rounds off the night nicely.

There are no rigid rules for when you can or cannot eat. Cafés and *confiterías* (larger, elegant and slightly old-fashioned cafés) are open throughout the day and well into the night – often all night. *Café con leche* and croissants are still served at three in the afternoon and you can order a toasted ham and cheese sandwich at 4:00 am should you so wish. Restaurants, on the other hand, will open for lunch, close during the afternoon and open again in the late evening for dinner.

Lunch takes place at about 1:00 pm. It may last several hours or be just a frantic sandwich grabbed while you can. Don't even think

Happy diners reflected in a mirror of a parrilla.

about going out for dinner, however, until at least 9:00 pm – and even that's considered early. Argentines eat late. When most restaurants throughout the rest of the world are wiping down their tables and bidding a weary farewell to their last customers, Argentines are just tucking into their first course and cracking open the *vino*. Ten, eleven, even midnight is a perfectly normal time to sit down to dinner. Even in the smallest of provincial towns, it's considered abnormal to go out for supper before 9:00 pm. (Nothing will be open anyway.) The same rules apply if you're eating in.

With at least eight hours between lunch and dinner, teatime is crucial. At 5:00 pm, cafés start filling up and orders are put in for more coffee and cake. This is the perfect time to eat *facturas* – delicious pastries stuffed with *dulce de leche*. Teatime is also a popular time to meet friends at home. If you are invited to someone's house for tea, do pop into a bakery on your way and bring a bag of *facturas* along with you.

Ordering

Waiters will respond to *camarero*, *che*, *mozo*, *flaco* and just about any other Argentine nickname, but you won't have to make much effort to get their attention as they are incredibly on the ball. Table waiting is a noble occupation in Argentina and customer service is generally impeccable. In the more traditional *confiterías*, waiters are invariably ancient men in bow ties and stiff white aprons with surprisingly steady hands. Occasionally, you can't help feeling as if you're being served by your grandfather and that perhaps you ought to leap up and help. But once you've seen Argentine waiters in action – young and old alike – you soon realise that you are in the hands of experts.

Just ordering a small espresso in a café becomes a mesmerising event. In a flurry of hands and silver trays, the waiter will deposit a napkin, a coaster, an ashtray, a complimentary glass of soda water, a plate of macaroons, white packets of sugar, pink packets of artificial sweetener, your coffee and finally the bill, skewered majestically onto a metal spike. The entire process takes just a few seconds. He deserves a round of applause, not to mention a tip!

For meals in restaurants, the bill won't be brought to you until you have finished your meal and asked for it. This is done by raising your hand and moving it around, as if you were writing in the air. But don't feel you have to rush. Argentines spend hours at the table, lingering over coffee after coffee, deep in discussion. Traditionally, this is a time when the whole family gathers together and discusses anything and everything. Waiters respect this tradition – known locally as the *sobremesa* – and won't boot you out to make space for new customers just because you've finished eating.

The only time a waiter's role becomes fairly redundant is at a *tenador libre* restaurant. For a set price of five to six dollars, *tenedor libres* (literally, 'free fork') let you eat as much as you want from an open buffet. This is wonderful value if you're especially hungry. Needless to say, they are exceptionally popular among gangs of ravenous young men who, much to the disdain of the restaurateur, manage to polish off more than their fair share of the goodies on offer.

SNACKING

Considering the enormous gap between lunch at about 1:00 pm and dinner some nine or ten hours later (and often no breakfast at all), snacking is not only an enjoyable Argentine tradition but one that is essential to survival. The most readily available snack to knock those hunger pains on the head is the *alfajor*, a crumbly fat biscuit sandwich filled with the eternally popular *dulce de leche* and bathed in chocolate. The smarter varieties often come coated in meringue.

Entire dynasties have been founded on the humble *alfajor*. Like fudge or rock in other counties, each region produces its own unique brand of *alfajor* and in practically every town throughout the country, you can buy your *alfajores* with quaint pictures of the local scenery on the box. It is also considered the perfect goodwill gesture and an ideal gift to bring your hostess.

Other snacks include the handy *empanada,* a cheese or meat pattie stuffed with olives and hardboiled egg, prodigious in the northwest and popular everywhere else. *Choripan* is a delicious spicy sausage split open and sandwiched between thick crusty white bread and available from every roadside stall. *Pancho* is the local term for a hot dog, a *super pancho* being an enormous hot dog. When winter starts to kick in, look out for *churros con chocolate. Churros* are long, fat, deep-fried doughy sticks, decadently stuffed with – you guessed it – *dulce de leche,* and the hot chocolate's so thick you can stand both your spoon – and the *churro* – up in it.

Meanwhile, if you want something to nibble on with your cold drink in a café ask the waiter for a *picada* – he or she will conjure up a small plate of crisps and nuts.

SHOPPING FOR FOOD

Most Argentines buy the bulk of their food from supermarkets, which are well stocked and found everywhere. These are wonderful en-claves for all sorts of Italian goodies such as pizza, mozzarella, tomato sauces and Parmesan cheese. There are entire aisles devoted to different pasta types alone. Then, of course, there is the meat section, manned by fierce-looking men in blood-spattered aprons, wielding hatchets. It's at the meat counter where you really do get an idea about the innards and offal that you've been happily gobbling at an *asado.* They don't make any effort to make these look pretty, and unless you have a strong stomach, steel yourself to see tongues hacked up and intestines unravelled.

Supermarkets are also often the best – and cheapest – places to buy wines and other drinks but the fruit and vegetable sections often look as if they could do with some cheering up. For these you're best off going to the specialist fresh fruit and vegetable stalls – usually cleverly located directly opposite the supermarket. In smaller towns, look out for fruit and vegetable wagons that are pulled around the streets. Likewise, supermarkets generally have a good bakery section, but for a greater selection and variety of breads and pastries go to a *panadería* (bakery).

Home delivery is also popular, especially for pizzas and *empanadas*. The deliverymen travel to your front door by motorbike, and in a land of motoring maniacs are some of the most dangerous on the road. They will expect a tip.

DRINK

Argentines guzzle gallons of soft drinks. The standard cola, Diet Coke and lemonade are everywhere but do look out for the local tonic water, *Paso de los Toros*, which also comes in a fizzy grapefruit (*pomelo*) flavour. And you won't be able to miss the local beer, *Quilmes*, which comes in cans and litre bottles.

The cheapest soft drink to order in a bar or restaurant is soda water. This normally arrives in old-fashioned soda bottles with metal or plastic siphons. Make sure you get the right pressure and angle when squeezing the handle. If not, you can easily soak yourself and your companions. Tap water is generally drinkable everywhere in Argentina but if you're worried or have a very sensitive stomach ask for mineral water – either fizzy (*agua con gas*) or still (*agua sin gas*).

All these drinks, however, come leagues behind in the popularity stakes after wine, coffee and *yerba mate*.

YERBA MATE

Mate (pronounced 'mat-ay') is a tea made from the leaves and stems of the *yerba mate* bush, which is related to holly and grows like a weed in the Paraná and Paraguay river basins. Its scientific name is *Ilex paraguarensis*, and it is also known as Paraguayan tea and Jesuit tea – apparently Jesuit missionaries in the 18th century were quite hooked on *mate* after being introduced to it by Guaraní Indians. In Argentina, however, it is always referred to as either *yerba mate* or simply *mate*.

Mate is a well-kept secret – it is commonly drunk only in Argentina, Paraguay, Uruguay and southern Brazil. Yet among the various merits of *I. paraguarensis* are its properties as a stimulant to the central nervous system, a diuretic, an anti-rheumatic and a tonic. In extremely large doses it causes purging and vomiting. Some herbalists have gone so far as to suggest that it can delay the signs of ageing (even stop you from going grey), reduce stress and stimulate your mind. One Argentine acquaintance who swears by its seduction potential gives girlfriends the ultimation, 'Darling, either we drink *mate* or we go to bed.' I guess sooner or later the poor girl has to give in or OD!

One thing's certain: *mate* drinking keeps the Argentines permanently on their toes. The active ingredient in *mate* is a powerful little alkaloid known as mateine which, to all intents and purposes, is identical to caffeine and packs the same punch. Here may well lie the secret of Argentines' ability to party night after night and be the key to becoming a true *trasnochador*.

Mate plays a key part in Argentine culture and at times you could be forgiven for thinking that the entire country is happily hooked on this mildly narcotic tea. The vast majority of Argentines won't go anywhere without their *mate* and a thermos flask for a ready supply of hot water. They are quick to point out, however, that they are not nearly as addicted as their friends in Uruguay, who are said to be quite capable of drinking *mate* and riding their bicycles at the same time, a thermos flask neatly tucked under their arm.

Still, many Argentines drink *mate* several times a day – as many as eight times a day in the countryside. To say that the Argentines love their *mate* is no exaggeration. There's even been tangos written about it – and in Argentina that's about as high as you can go.

Drinking the Stuff

A wooden gourd (also confusingly known as a *mate*) is stuffed with *yerba mate* and filled with hot, but *never* boiling or boiled, water. The resulting tea is drunk through a metal, often silver, straw known as a *bombilla*. At first, this strikes you as ludicrous as the water that's poured into the *mate* is just off boiling point and the *bombilla* quickly gets red hot and sticks to your lower lip. It may even give the inexperienced mate drinker a blister. Once you get the knack, by which time you'll probably be as addicted as the next Argentine, you won't want to drink it any cooler. (Although Paraguayans, and some Argentines from the north, drink their *mate* ice-cold, as *tereré* – much to the amusement and horror of the rest of Argentina.)

Yerba mate can be bought in kilos everywhere in Argentina under various brand names. A kilo costs about US$3 and should keep a family of four happily wired for about a week. Essential *mate* drinking paraphernalia – a thermos flask (to store the hot water), a *bombilla* and the *mate* gourd – can be purchased cheaply in supermarkets and thrift stores throughout the country. Some *bombillas* and *mates* can be very elaborate affairs: ornate silver-plated antique *mates* and *bombillas* can fetch hundreds of dollars. *Mates* also come in all sorts of different shapes and sizes. They are made from calabashes, aromatic wood and even out of bull's testicles!

Drinking *mate* is a very social affair; mate is usually drunk among friends and family gathered together at home. One *mate* is passed round and round a group. Each person drinks the full serving before passing it back to be refilled by the 'server', who then passes it on again. As you can imagine, the mateine kick sparks up the already chatty Argentines no end. It's an endless circle – the more *mate* you drink the more you talk, and the more you talk the longer you stay drinking *mate*.

For these reasons alone, you should never turn down an opportunity to drink *mate*. But be warned – the first time you try it, however adventurous your taste buds, you'll probably find it revolting. 'It always tastes like someone's spat into it,' said one acquaintance. 'It was like putting my lips round an exhaust pipe,' said another about the *bombilla*. Unaccustomed drinkers have described *mate* as tasting like earth, bonfire smoke, withered leaves and boiled straw. One visitor thought that they were doing drugs!

Drinking mate in Santa Cruz province, deepest Patagonia.

The best advice is to persevere and you should come to love and revere it as much as the Argentines. In the process you will provide your hosts with lots of amusement at the vision of a gringo drinking *mate*. Personally, after months of perseverance, I'm now as hooked as the next Argentine and can't contemplate a day without a *mate* hit.

139

Mate Etiquette

The *mate* ritual is rather reminiscent of a Native American peace pipe ceremony. An offer of *mate* is a sign of friendship and to be included in a round of *mate* means that you have been accepted. No self-respecting Argentine would dream of drinking *mate* on his own without offering it around to everyone else in the room. If an Argentine offers you a *mate* you may feel that you can congratulate yourself on having got this far.

But don't sit back and relax just yet. An amazing and intricate set of rules and regulations revolves around the art of *mate* drinking. Commit a *mate faux pas* now and you could blow your chances at impressing your new friends – not to mention becoming a laughing stock.

The first thing you should be aware of is saying, or rather not saying, thank you. Most of us when offered a drink will automatically be inclined to thank our host. But if you thank an Argentine who has just handed you a *mate*, it will be taken as a 'no thank you'. You will be excluded from the next round and may end up feeling left out. If you really feel that you can't just accept a drink without saying something, try murmuring an appreciative comment instead, perhaps something like 'yum, how delicious' or 'great *mate* this'. But *never* say thank you, unless of course you don't want any more.

Once you have accepted a *mate*, you will be expected to drink all of it. There's no room for halfhearted measures in the *mate* ritual. The problem, however, is that you will probably take one mouth-scalding boiled straw sip and your instinct will be to hand it back quickly to wherever it came from. To do so would be to commit a grave social blunder, akin to giving someone your mangy leftovers. You will know when you have drunk all the liquid because the *bombilla* will make a loud gurgling slurpy noise as you come to the end – it should sound rather like the noise that is made as you suck up the dregs of a milkshake through a straw. Only once you've made the 'milkshake slurp' can you pass the *mate* back.

This leads us to another potential *mate* minefield. Faced with the prospect of having to down the entire blisteringly hot drink in one fell swoop, you may be tempted to play for time in the hope that the drink will cool off or someone will take it away from you – basically doing anything to distract from the matter in hand. This is considered awfully bad manners. One should never 'sit' on the *mate* for too long; ideally you should finish the entire drink in as few slurps as possible without ever putting it down on the table and quickly hand it back to your host. (Some *mates* are designed with a round bottom so that they cannot be put down.) By sitting on the *mate*, you become a '*mate* hog' and are not entering into the spirit of the *mate* ritual.

Occasionally, in a futile attempt to cool down the *mate*, unaccustomed *mate* drinkers play around with the *bombilla*. Don't be tempted! The *bombilla* stays put, whatever. On no account should you pull it out or, worse still, try and stir the *mate*. Should you do so, you will be greeted by horrified gasps and the *mate* will be snatched away from you immediately, as if you were a small toddler making icky messes with his food.

Once you finish the *mate*, you should always hand it back to the *cebador* (the person who prepared the *mate*), who will then refill it and pass it on to the next person in the round.

Mate Talk

Mate involves a very subtle language. You should be aware of this so you don't send out unintentional messages, or worse still, not get the message yourself. If a *mate* is blocked – you can't drink it because the *bombilla* is clogged with little particles – then literally speaking it means you're not welcome and should take it as an insult. Unfortunately, however, if a *mate* has been badly prepared this happens quite frequently and it's probably meant unintentionally. If you overfill or spill the *mate*, however, the next person to drink from it will soon be cuckolded. Of course, unless you really are very superstitious, you should take these signs with a pinch of salt.

Mate is often mixed with various ingredients such as milk or honey and these too may carry hidden messages. Only serious *mate* drinkers, however, will still take the following traditional gaucho sayings seriously:

bitter *mate*	indifference
sweet *mate*	friendship/welcome
mate with balm	I'm angry with you
mate with cinnamon	I'm interested in you
mate with lemon	I'd rather not see you
mate with burnt sugar	I'm thinking of you
mate with orange peel	come and find me
mate with elisa	your sadness grieves me
mate with milk	esteem, respect
mate with coffee	I was angry but now I forgive you
mate with honey	marriage

Seven Easy Steps in Preparing Mate

The *matero*, or any keen *mate* drinker, should have the art of preparing a *mate* down to a T. Here are seven pointers that should turn you into an ace *matero*:

- Fill the *mate* (gourd) to about two-thirds full with *yerba mate*.
- Cover the top of the *mate* with your hand and shake it gently upside down. This forces the smaller particles to the top so that they don't get sucked up and clog the *bombilla*.
- Pour hot water (around 80°C), never boiling or boiled water, gently into the *mate* at the edge of the gourd near the *bombilla*, until it rises to the top. If you've done it right, a froth should cover the surface.
- Let the *mate* stand a few seconds. It may need a little top-up the first time as the dry *mate* leaves absorb the water. But be careful not to overfill.
- Close the *bombilla's* mouthpiece with your thumb and insert it firmly into the *mate*. From now on, do not move it again, play with it or pull it out even when refilling with water. And *never* stir.

- If you prepare the *mate*, you must take the first drink, which is normally very bitter and strong. As the *cebador*, it will be your duty to refill the *mate* with water each time and pass it on.
- If the *mate* loses its foaminess and you can see little bits of stalk floating on the surface, then your *mate* is *lavado* (washed) and will have lost its taste. To avoid a *mate* becoming *lavado* – which will happen eventually if you go a lot of rounds – add a little more *yerba mate* every three or four servings.

Curing and Caring for Your Mate

If you buy a brand new *mate* gourd – which is likely as an Argentine will be reluctant to part with his – your *mate* just won't taste the same until your gourd's been weathered, or cured. To do this, you must fill your newly purchased gourd with used *yerba mate*, add hot water and let it stand for a day. The next day remove all the *mate*, rinse the gourd and scrape out any soft tissue. Repeat the whole process. You may need to do this for several days. As long as you're still scraping out soft tissue, your gourd is not completely cured and any *mate* served in it will taste unusually bitter.

It is a cardinal sin to clean your gourds with detergent; the *mate* would be tainted with a soapy flavour for weeks. Simply rinse out the *mate* with cold water and let it stand to dry. *Bombillas* should be cleaned regularly so that the sievelike end doesn't become clogged with little particles. Many *bombillas* can be dismantled to make cleaning easier.

Strangely enough, despite its universal popularity, you won't be able to order a *mate* in a restaurant or café. The closest you can get is a *mate cocido* which is *mate* leaves in a tea bag. Cafés are normally reserved for the second national drink: coffee.

Café Society

When it comes to caffeine consumption, the Argentines are unbeatable. Decaffeinated coffee is practically unheard of and there's even a popular brand of aspirin – *cafiaspirina* – which is laced with high quantities of caffeine and boldly claims to soothe headaches, combat colds and boost your spirits.

In the quest to be spiced with caffeine, Argentines across the country have perfected coffee houses into an art form. You must also remember that this is a nationality that simply adores chatting, and what could be nicer than chatting over steaming coffee in one of Argentina's justifiably famous cafés?

Argentine society is a café society at heart, and a great deal of time is spent dawdling over cups of coffee in the country's cafés and *confiterías*. There is at least one café on the corner of each block and usually a few more in between. If you want to meet up with someone, you arrange a rendezvous not at the office or on a street corner, but in a café. As a result, cafés are generally packed throughout the day and well into the night. It's also totally acceptable to sit on your own in a café at any time of the day or night – no pitying looks will be forthcoming and you'll be left in peace.

After all, cafés are there to be sat in. It's practically impossible to get a coffee in a polystyrene cup to 'take away'. You can, however, order a coffee to be brought to your office. An efficient waiter will leave the café, cross the street and serve you coffee in a proper cup on a silver tray at your desk, then return and take away the cup once you've finished.

Coffee comes in all sorts of varieties, the most popular being the *café cortado* – a lethally strong espresso cut with a shot of steamed milk. Argentines like their coffee sweet and will heap up to five spoonfuls of sugar into a coffee cup that is marginally larger than a thimble. If you take your coffee unsweetened, brace yourself for some bemused looks. As well as the *cortado*, there are cappuccinos (which come topped with cream and chocolate powder), espressos (black and potent) and *café con leche* – a large milky coffee that's ideal at breakfast. Most coffees arrive with a complimentary glass of soda water and little macaroon-like biscuits.

Suffice to say, caffeine consumption, be it from *mate*, coffee or *cafiaspirina*, keeps most Argentines wired most of the time.

WINE

Just as they are hugely proud of their *bife*, Argentines are also prone to bragging that they produce some of the best wine in the world, and to prove it (until very recently) they drank it all themselves. By the late 1970s the average Argentine was putting away an astonishing 91 litres of wine a year. It does go well with beef!

Thanks to this insatiable domestic market, Argentina found itself with nothing left over to export and that is probably why you've seen more Chilean wines on the supermarket shelves back at home. But all this is changing. Argentina is now the fourth largest producer of wine in the world and although local consumption is still considerable (today Argentines boast the world's third largest per capita consumption of wine), there's a lot more Argentine wine entering the international market.

Not that this needs to concern you if you are actually in Argentina and have joined the ranks of the happy domestic wine guzzling market, where you can pick up a decent bottle of *vino* for little more than a dollar.

Choosing a Wine

Argentine wines range from very good to very rough, and if you don't have any local guidance, buying wine can turn into a bit of a lottery. Still, when a bottle of wine can cost the same as a litre of cola, the key is experimentation.

Wines in Argentina are divided into two categories: noble wines or fine wines known as *vino fino* and cheaper table wines known as *vino comun* or *vino de mesa*.

By law, only *vino fino* can be put into the small three-quarter litre bottles. *Vino comun* goes into litre bottles or boxes, and into the phenomenal five-litre containers.

Whether an Argentine wine is *comun* or *fino* has nothing to do with the price – although *vino fino* is generally more expensive (over US$3) and *vino comun* can be as cheap as US$1 a bottle. Rather it has to do with the type of grape from which the wine is made. There are very strict regulations as to what grapes can be used in different areas of the country for different types of wine.

You also won't find a *vino comun* which is varietal – in other words made from one single type of grape. It will usually be a mixture of fairly cheap grapes to make a cheap wine.

Grape varieties grown in Argentina include Malbec, Torrontés, Chardonnay, Chenin, Riesling, Sauvignon, Cabernet Sauvignon and Merlot. But it's really the Malbec (a red) and the Torrontés (a white) that are taking the world by storm. These two shouldn't be missed. (But you shouldn't confine yourself to them either.)

The Vineyards

Argentina's vineyards flourish in the Mendoza region – which produces over 70 per cent of all Argentine wines – but there are also vineyards in San Juan, Salta, La Rioja and Río Negro provinces. Argentina takes full advantage of the extraordinarily dry climate throughout the Andean region which allows just the right amount of humidity and water that the vines need. A further plus for Argentine wines is that they are made from very natural, clean and healthy grapes. In a bad year, grapes are only sprayed twice, compared with 10 or 12 times in Chile and even more in Brazil.

Quite a number of vineyards and wineries (*bodegas*) are well worth a visit and all will welcome you with open arms and bottles. To mention just a couple, try Chandon, with its fantastic sparkling wine installation, or Norton's picturesque old-style winery, both in Mendoza. For a more picturesque and exotic setting, visit the vineyards in the whitewashed colonial-style town of Cafayate, Salta.

If you want to catch the grape harvest, aim to visit a vineyard between the second half of February and the first half of April. But

Enough bottles of vino in this bodega to keep Cafayate's locals and visitors happy for weeks!

from an aesthetic point of view, the spring months of October and November are great. And if you love autumn colours, April is a fantastic month, when the vineyards are all browns, russets and golds, surrounded by poplars with snow on the lower mountains as a spectacular backdrop. *Salud!*

Chapter Seven

FOOTBALL AND OTHER RELIGIONS

'Boca is my heart's joy. You're my life, you're my passion, more than anything. It doesn't matter where you play, I'll come and see you at home or away. Not even death will separate us, I'll support you from heaven.'

—Boca Juniors football song

On the whole, Argentines take a fairly laid-back approach to religion. (Real Sunday worship, they joke, takes place on the football pitch, even if the hordes of fans yelling and jumping around in the stands are anything but saintly.) Church congregations are considerably smaller than you'd imagine in a country where 90 per cent of the population are Roman Catholic. In fact, less than 20 per cent of Argentina's Catholics are actively practising. A running joke claims that the rest of the country only goes to church for weddings and funerals!

But although the church pews aren't as packed as they could be on Sundays, few Argentines would ever dream of calling themselves atheists. On the contrary, religious beliefs run deep and form a very integral part of many Argentines' lives. Try and visit Luján, where a statue of the beloved patron saint of Argentina – the Virgin of Luján – is on display in the imposing twin-spired Gothic basilica. Sooner or later, most Argentines will make the trip to Luján which sees more than four million pilgrims a year. Many of Argentina's Catholics will also make the sign of the cross when they pass churches, cathedrals or religious altars. This can be especially nerve-wracking if you pass a church at high speed in a car, as it involves drivers removing their hands from the steering wheel to cross themselves.

Cars, buses and trucks are especially laden down with religious symbols. Hanging plastic rosaries weigh down rear-view mirrors and glittery stickers of the Madonna are glued onto windscreens (sometimes rather sacrilegiously next to pictures of scantily clad girls). A newspaper poll once revealed that most Argentines believe car crashes to be 'unavoidable acts of God'. Out of this comes another popular joke: 'A priest and a taxi driver arrive at the gates of heaven but St Peter lets only the taxi driver enter. The priest asks St Peter, "Why didn't you let me go in too?" St Peter replies, "When you said mass nobody prayed, but when that taxi driver drove – everybody prayed!"'

Although Catholicism is the official state religion, freedom of worship is written into the constitution. In addition to the Catholic majority, there are small religious groups, of which the main groups, Protestants and Jews, form 2 per cent of the population each. There is also an ever-growing Evangelical movement. (The city of Ushuaia in Tierra del Fuego, to take an exceptional example, has 12 Evangelical churches and only one Catholic church.)

HOME-GROWN RELIGION

At first sight, Argentines appear to be fairly straightforward Catholics. But if you delve a little deeper, you will see deviations. An example might be the hand-painted sign above the holy water in Salta's colonial cathedral warning visitors, 'Don't throw it on the floor, don't use it as a remedy and don't use it for acts of witchcraft.'

As with the rest of Latin America, the Catholic faith that was brought over with the Spaniards over time incorporated many of the indigenous traditions. Although far from the scale of what happened in, for example, Bolivia or Mexico, Argentina has its share of unconventional rituals and ceremonies, especially in the country's northwestern provinces. In the Humahuaca valley, religious festivals may include ceremonies for the more pagan Andean earth mother (Pachamama).

The Strange Legend of La Difunta Correa

One of Argentina's strangest religious offshoots is the cult of La Difunta Correa. La Difunta – literally 'the deceased' – is the name given to Deolinda Correa who set out on foot with her infant son to follow her husband's battalion during the civil war in the 1840s. She eventually succumbed to hunger and thirst in the desert of San Juan. Yet when a group of soldiers stumbled upon her dead body some days later, to their amazement they discovered her baby son still nursing at her breast – alive and well. A miracle was declared and La Difunta Correa became an overnight legend. It wasn't long before a shrine emerged just outside the small desert hamlet of Vallecito where her remains are buried.

A shrine to La Difunta Correa in Vallecito.

Strange stuff indeed, but La Difunta has to be doing something right or she wouldn't have so many admirers nor such an incalculable number of thank you presents given to her by grateful Argentines who have asked for and apparently received her help. Thousands of Argentines make a pilgrimage to the grave in Vallecito each year where they leave La Difunta gifts and plastic bottles of water in thanks for miracles granted in her name. Literally hundreds of roadside shrines to La Difunta have been erected alongside the country's highways from Iguazú to southern Patagonia where long-distance truck drivers leave her the usual plastic bottles of water beside what look suspiciously like vital parts of their engines.

In Vallecito, bedazzling shrines have sprung up around her grave filled with gifts that could stock a large department store. These are no ordinary trinkets but incredibly precious and personal stuff. Among some of La Difunta's more spectacular thank you presents are ponchos from Ecuador, a doll from Japan, a Black Virgin from Zaire, giant Mexican sombreros and a troop of stuffed penguins from Patagonia. There are also electric guitars, university degrees, a bandoneon, an enormous double bass, hockey sticks, paddle rackets, tennis rackets, military swords, wedding rings, china plates, chainsaws and a rather motheaten stuffed Pekinese.

Perhaps the strangest shrine to La Difunta is filled with wedding paraphernalia, given by newlyweds who believe that they have La Difunta to thank for tying the knot. Racks of bridal gowns – surely a woman's most treasured possession – have been given to La Difunta and overflow from glass cabinets. On the walls are photographs of blushing brides next to nervous looking grooms, and photocopies of wedding certificates.

'What's on display is only a fraction of what we have,' Gladys Heredia, administrator of the Vallecito site, told me before flinging open the doors of an enormous hangar stacked with hundreds of bicycles, cars, motorbikes and trucks left by more of La Difunta's admirers.

La Difunta's supernatural powers and her enormous following are proving to be a headache for Argentina's Catholic hierarchy who, in spite of regular petitions, have refused point-blank to recognise La Difunta as an object of veneration.

'We tried to get the Pope to make her a saint,' said a slightly miffed Gladys. 'But he won't.'

The Grateful Dead

La Difunta Correa's shrine in the San Juan desert is just one of many graves across the country that attracts Argentines in their swarms. In fact veneration of the dead is so widespread in Argentina that the Argentines have once been described – somewhat alarmingly – as 'cadaver cultists'.

With a trip to the local cemetery seen as a perfectly normal thing to do on an afternoon out, you may feel that you've stumbled across something out of the Addams Family. But death is big business in Argentina. There's nothing like the death of a famous Argentine to unite the country. When tango star and budding actor Carlos Gardel was cut down in his prime after the plane he was travelling in crashed in Colombia, the nation was beside itself with grief. And after Evita Perón died of cancer in 1952, huge numbers of the nation sank into uncontrollable grief – some distraught mourners had to be physically restrained from poisoning themselves at the foot of her glass coffin on display in the labour ministry. National heroes such as the great liberator General José de San Martín are remembered by the day of their death rather than their birth or for dates of historic greatness. And pilgrimages to the graves of the dead, both relatives and the famous, are a popular national pastime.

Even if cemeteries give you the creeps, you shouldn't miss out on a chance to join in this national fixation and take a peek into one of Argentina's famous necropolises. Not only do they provide fascinatingly morbid viewing, they are also a surprising source of insight into Argentine society itself.

Every town and village, however small, throughout the country has its own cemetery. The larger cemeteries are cities in themselves, with paved streets, tree-lined avenues and family tombs in every conceivable architectural style from Neoclassical to Art Nouveau, Gothic to Romantic. Inside these 'cities of the dead', tombs and mausoleums are crammed shoulder to shoulder along a maze of streets and passages. Chacarita cemetery in Buenos Aires, which is considered the largest urban cemetery in the world, is so vast that mourners can drive up to the tomb doors on numbered streets with parking spaces or buy a cup of coffee from one of the cemetery's peddlers. It is slightly incongruous to see men in suits driving up to tombs with bunches of flowers as if dropping in on a lover rather than a dead relative. You need an acute sense of direction, or better still a map, to avoid getting lost in Chacarita. And unless you ask a lurking undertaker for directions, you can only hope to stumble across the tomb you're looking for.

Claustrophobia sufferers should steer well clear of the narrower passages in Argentina's cemeteries. And if cobwebs, lace and coffins aren't your thing, then don't go peering too closely through the windows or, for that matter, go alone! Particularly creepy are the older tombs that have fallen into decay, where some coffin lids lie at awkward angles. These mausoleums will eventually be reclaimed and sold to new families – 'out with the old and in with the new', so to speak. Popular cemeteries have seen something of a boom in real estate prices. In Recoleta cemetery in the heart of Buenos Aires, tomb space goes for as much as US$70,000 for a few square metres, making this effectively one of the most expensive plots of land in the world.

The cemetery of Recoleta lies in the heart of Barrio Norte, among the boutiques, cafés and marble-halled apartments of Buenos Aires' richest and most fashionable neighbourhood. This in itself speaks for the importance of death in Argentine society – surely there aren't many other towns in the world with the claim that the closer you live to the cemetery, the smarter your address?

Tales from the Crypt

The recent appearance of a cemetery guide in Spanish, English, French and Portuguese confirmed La Recoleta cemetery as the city's number one tourist attraction. Plaques on the tombs read like an Argentine *Who's Who* with a dazzling string of former presidents, generals, poets and socialites. A short twirl around the cemetery is like skipping across the pages of a book on Argentine history.

Indeed, so sought after is a slot in Recoleta, a local adage has it that you haven't really made it in Argentina if your remains don't end up there. There are 6,500 family tombs in Recoleta with an average of 15 bodies in each so, as well as expensive, Recoleta is also rather crowded. At night, just to add an even more macabre dimension, the place also seethes with cats.

This may all seem a little too close for comfort, if not a tad unhygienic to have in the very centre of the city, but the Argentines like to have their dead heroes close by. After Carlos Gardel died in Colombia, his corpse travelled halfway round the world – by way of New York, Rio de Janeiro and Montevideo – before being buried in Chacarita cemetery. His grave is one of the most colourful in the cemetery and the life-size statue of the *tanguero* that rises above his

Photo: Jamie Grant

A lion stands guard in front of a family tomb in Recoleta.

grave is regularly visited by fans who leave flowers and provide a steady supply of lit cigarettes in the statue's hand.

In 1989, President Menem went to great lengths to bring back the remains of Juan Manuel de Rosas – the bloodthirsty gaucho warlord – to Argentina. Understandably, the Argentines were mortified when their famous poet and writer, Jorge Luis Borges, refused to join the afterlife Argentine rat race, opting instead for Geneva's Cimetiere des Rois for his burial place. A controversial tug of war is still going on to bring him back to Recoleta.

Someone that the dead oligarchs of Recoleta would probably prefer not to be in their midst is Evita Perón. Her sombre black marble mausoleum is the cemetery's most visited grave – mainly from devoted *peronistas* and curious tourists who've seen the movie with Madonna in the lead role. It took the Spanish embalmer Dr Pedro Ara an entire year to make Evita's body indestructible. (His work was said to have driven him crazy and it is even rumoured that he may have performed ungodly acts with Evita's body.) One thing's for sure, no one can get near Evita now. Her coffin lies beneath 12 inches of steel plate inside the Familia Duarte tomb with bulletproof doors and is said to be able to survive a nuclear attack.

Perón himself is buried on the other side of town in Chacarita cemetery. One afternoon I ended up in front of Perón's tomb where I was joined by three women mourners who it turned out were praying not for him, but to him. Their prayers began, 'Señor Perón, who art in heaven.' These were clearly committed *peronistas* who had come to pay their respects and admire the hundreds of wreaths that had been left there the day before on the anniversary of his death. When she thought no one was looking, I saw one of the women surreptitiously pluck a rose from a filigree frame and tuck it away in her handbag as a precious keepsake.

The Curious World of Cemetery Caretakers

During the day, Argentina's top cemeteries swarm with an army of caretakers who are paid by relatives to clean and maintain the family tomb. In Recoleta cemetery almost 100 people do the job. Among them is Francisco, who proved a most enlightened if not peculiar tour guide.

'Ghosts, pah! This is the most peaceful place on earth. Let's drink *mate*,' he declared heartily and led me into a nearby tomb where his *mate* kettle was boiling on a camping stove. Perched on a coffin lid we drank our *mate* while Francisco, who like most Argentines boomed rather than spoke, divulged the secrets of Recoleta with what could only be described as cheerful glee. Later we entered all the different mausoleums. Inside one he told me he took siestas there in the summer where it was nice and cool – a superstitious sort would have pegged this extraordinary caretaker for a vampire. He wore a glossy black velvet suit opened to reveal a sparkling medallion nestled on a blanket of chest hair. His smile was dazzling and our conversation was frequently interrupted by the shrill of a mobile phone that dangled

157

from a holster on his belt. Dark glasses completed the ensemble. 'I'm at my happiest here,' he said, tapping the lid of the coffin. 'Cemeteries aren't just for the dead, you know.'

A FOOTBALL-MAD NATION

Football is, without doubt, what really drives the Argentines to fever pitch. Forget Mass or even a famous death, *this* is Argentina's universal religion. Football players acquire an almost godlike status. Top players and team managers form a key part of Argentina's *farándula* or jet set, often dating models and actresses. In fact, Argentine football players are stars in their own right – Diego Maradona's sex, drug and rock 'n' roll antics have kept the paparazzi in business for years.

In Argentina, football (soccer to North Americans) is more of an institution than just a game. No one can be a mere passive spectator. Fans tend to strip to the waist (male ones anyway) and paint their faces in their team's colours. Flares, firecrackers, smoke bombs and gunpowder along with endless singing all create stupendous noise levels, while streams of tickertape are hurled down from the stands onto the pitch below. Often tear gas and plastic bullets are added to the general commotion by police stationed to keep things under control. Some of the more fanatical supporters go armed with knives and guns, which they aren't afraid to whip out should they encounter the opposition. In fact, as one cynical commentator put it, 'Argentina is about the only country in the world where people are prepared to kill each other over a football game.'

Key games are often brought forward to Friday and Saturday evenings – as well as the ubiquitous Sunday afternoon slot – for optimum televised viewing. During these times all eyes not in the stadium itself are lovingly glued to TV screens. And you can't escape the fervour over a quiet *café con leche* down the street. Every cantina and café throughout the country will also be showing the game at top volume with the customers letting out huge synchronised cheers when their team scores a goal or even rushing out onto the sidewalk to let off fireworks and ear-splitting bangers. If the game has been particularly spectacular, fans will take to the streets in their hordes, banging drums or driving round and round the plaza honking their car horns. It's probably the closest thing you get to tribal warfare in Argentina.

This obsession with football is encouraged from an early age. A football is generally the first toy a baby boy is given, usually when he's just a few months old. By the time they've reached school age, many boys dream of playing one day for a premier division team or, better still, the National Squad. 'For practically all Argentine boys, football is a madness and playing is the thing that interests them the most,' says José-Luis Barrios, a commentator at *El Gráfico* sports magazine. 'It's the most popular sport in the country by far. It's an Argentine passion.'

No open space is left unused. Empty car lots are transformed into impromptu football pitches at the weekends, lampposts double up as goal posts and the walls of telephone booths become heated arenas of a graffiti war between various teams. It is no exaggeration to say that Argentine men literally spend hours talking about football. If you pass a group of guys deep in conversation you can bet that it's probably not about girls, cars or even pizza. They will be talking football. This leads to the popular local saying that wives don't have husbands on Sunday afternoons. Mind you, I've also known women to drop everything when a River-Boca game comes on television.

El Clásico: Boca vs River

Two teams dominate Argentina's cutthroat football scene: Boca Juniors and River Plate, better known as just 'Boca' and 'River'. Both teams are from Buenos Aires which has undoubtedly intensified the legendary rivalry. And even if you support another team for the rest of the year, when these two battle it out on the pitch, you're going to take sides. The fanaticism is infectious.

Excitable Boca fans during a football match.

River supporters.

A Boca-River game is known as *El Clásico* – 'The Classic' – and it's easy to see why. As equally matched archenemies, a game between these two giants temporarily splits the country in two. Between them, Boca and River can claim almost two-thirds of the country as fans. A recent study revealed that 32 per cent of Argentines support Boca, and 30 per cent are River fans.

But it's the Boca Junior fan who is the most vociferous and passionate. *'La mitad mas uno'* – 'half the country plus one,' say Boca fans about the supporters. And although this is not strictly true, judging by noise levels alone, you may at times believe it. Many Boca fans come from the same background as their former star player, Diego Maradona, whose family were poor immigrants mixed with Indian stock. For them, football is an escape valve, something to believe in. Their home ground is the square-shaped Bombonera stadium in the traditionally working-class Italian neighbourhood of La Boca. *Bombonera* means 'chocolate box' in Spanish but, as writer

Jimmy Burns points out, 'there is nothing sweet or contained about the scene'. When there's lots of singing and stamping – as is usual practice – the whole stadium shakes.

River fans may be marginally quieter than Boca's, but are equally fond of chucking tickertape and letting off fireworks and no less fanatical. As my friend Juan Luciano, a keen River supporter, pointed out, 'If I have a son and he supports Boca, I'd probably disinherit him.'

Bad Losers and Hooligans

What makes Argentina's football scene stand out so much more than other Latin countries', which are also known for their extreme passion for the game, are the highly organised and violent hooligan groups known as the *barra bravas* lurking behind the scenes. The *barra bravas* are the Argentine equivalent of football hooligans but are even more sinister in that they are seemingly above the law, despite being blatantly involved in drug-dealing, intimidation and even murder. In short, they're a nasty bunch.

'We all know who they are,' says Barrios from *El Gráfico*. 'They go to the stadiums with drugs and weapons. In a multitude of 40 or 50 thousand they are no more than 200 or 300 but that's enough to cause conflict.'

The *barra bravas* are there to do the dirty work. Club leaders may owe them favours or ask favours of them. The *barra bravas* act as the 'heavies'. For example, club leaders may encourage their *barra bravas* to threaten those who want to participate in club elections against them. They use them as personal bodyguards or to stick up posters. It's not unheard of for the *barra bravas* to go to a training session and threaten players of their own team who are playing badly or intimidate a trainer into resignation. At games, they are the fiercest supporters, often armed with knives, guns or just sheer brute force. They're largely responsible for selling drugs in the stands, robbery and even nastier crimes. In 1994, Boca *barra bravas* ambushed a truckload of River supporters after losing to them at La Bombonera.

In the ensuing onslaught the *barra bravas* shot dead two River supporters.

Violence at football matches is becoming an increasing concern for the authorities. (At one stage all second division matches were temporarily banned by a judge because he thought that the violence had got out of control.) One sad result is that women and young children are now quite a rare sight at football matches.

Surviving a Football Match

Given this powerful and intimidating combination of the bloodthirsty *barra bravas* and a general atmosphere that borders on mass hysteria, you may think twice before rushing off to see a football match. Still, if you do decide to go – and if you really want to get to grips with Argentine culture, you should experience at least one match – take note of the following pointers and try to tag along with someone local who'll know the scene.

- **Jump when everyone else jumps.** Concentrate on staying on your feet at all times and don't lose your balance. 'It was the closest thing to a heavy metal mosh pit I've come across since I've lived in Argentina, much more so than a Metallica concert,' said a Californian friend about a Racing vs Huracán match he'd seen. 'If you don't jump when everyone else does, you're going to get trampled.'
- **Seats or stands?** Seats (*plateas*) are safer than stands (*populares*) and more expensive. But it's in the stands where the passion is really felt. You decide.
- **Leave your Rolex at home.** Don't tempt fate and wear an expensive watch or jewellery or, for that matter, bring your wallet along with you, just enough cash to see you back home.
- **Stick to neutral colours.** Unless, of course, you're looking for trouble. You don't want to be the only one wearing blue in a sea of red.

Argentina's Top 20 Teams and Their Colours

Boca Juniors – yellow/dark blue
River Plate – white with diagonal red stripe
Independiente – all red
Racing Club – light blue and white stripes (like the national colours)
San Lorenzo – blue and red vertical stripes
Huracán – white with red collar
Argentinos Juniors – all red
Ferrocarril Oeste – green
Vélez Sarsfield – white with blue 'V'
Lanus – burgundy
Platense – white with dark brown stripes
Colón (Santa Fe) – half black, half red
Unión (Santa Fe) – red and white stripes
Rosario Central (Rosario) – yellow and blue stripes
Newell's Old Boys (Rosario) – half black, half red like Colón
Gimnasia y Esgrima (Jujuy) – white and light blue
Talleres (Córdoba) – dark blue and white vertical stripes
Belgrano (Córdoba) – light blue
Estudiantes (La Plata) – red and white stripes
Gymnasio (La Plata) – white and dark blue
(All teams are from Buenos Aires, unless otherwise stated.)

ENGLISH PIRATES AND THE MALVINAS (FALKLAND ISLANDS)

'There are two things that have truly united this country recently,' an Argentine friend confided. 'When we won the 1986 World Cup in Mexico and the day we invaded the Malvinas.' Both events, one football and the other war, in the space of just four years brought on an unprecedented outpouring of nationalist sentiment which saw hundreds of thousands of Argentines taking to the streets in celebration. And while football may be the overriding passion in Argentina, the potential for the Malvinas to stir up patriotic fervour is never far behind. In a country of immigrants that is in so many other ways disjointed, the Malvinas are a symbol of national identity: the fact that they were 'unfairly usurped by English pirates in 1833' is one of the few opinions that most Argentines wholeheartedly agree on.

If you plan to spend any time in Argentina, you should get wise about Las Malvinas. This obscure group of islands is probably better known to the rest of the English-speaking world as the Falkland Islands. Yet, in Argentina, the Falkland Islands are never referred to as the Falkland Islands, even by the most committed Anglophiles. They are known as Las Malvinas, just as Port Stanley, the capital, is known as nothing other than Puerto Argentino.

The Malvinas consist of two main islands and about 200 small islets, which together add up to an area no larger than Wales, lying some 480 kilometres off the shore of southern Patagonia in the South Atlantic Ocean. Treeless and barren, the mainstay of the economy for the 1,800 islanders – known by the Argentines as kelpers after the local seaweed – is sheep (all 650,000 of them).

The history of these small windswept bastions of the South Atlantic has a lot to answer for in the current international wrangle. Although the first undisputed sighting of the islands was by a Dutchman in 1598, the first people to actually settle on the Falklands/ Malvinas were probably French fishermen who established a garrison on East Falkland in 1764. Unknown to either the French or Spanish – who claimed the islands as part of the 1494 Treaty of Tordesillas that split the New World between Spain and Portugal – the British soon established an outpost on West Falkland at Port Egmont. When the Spanish discovered what was going on in East Falkland, they amicably bought out the French and established their own settlement and penal colony. Later, when they discovered the British in West Falkland, they kicked them out too, in 1770. A year later, and under threat of war, the Port Egmont outpost was reestablished by the British who abandoned the outpost in 1774, but not their territorial claims. Spanish forces also withdrew from the islands during the wars of independence (1810–20) but by 1820 the islands were once again resettled by an Argentine expedition from Buenos Aires. An incident involving sealers from the United States operating in the area piqued British interest sufficiently so that in 1833 British forces expelled the Argentine colony and brought the islands under British rule. Since then, the islands have been officially ruled by the British but unrelentingly claimed by the Argentines. For the Argentines, this isn't so much a question of right or wrong. It's just a fundamental and unshakeable belief that the islands were, are and always will be theirs.

The first thing any visitor to Argentina will probably read will be the words *Las Malvinas son Argentinas* – 'The Malvinas are Argentine'. This mantra is strategically placed on signposts at every port of entry. The sign catches the sunlight in the extreme north on the Bolivian border at nearly 4,000 meters above sea level. It is there at the steamy Iguazú falls for anyone who might come across from Brazil. You may see it along the ridge of the Andes at the Chilean frontier and, just in case you arrived by plane, it appears on billboards above the motorway that brings you in from Ezeiza airport.

If these reminders aren't enough, all maps in Argentina show the Falkland Islands in the national colours of light blue. If the maps are imported, then Falkland Is. (GB) will have been scratched out and replaced with Las Malvinas (Arg). The claim is so intrinsic that the islands are religiously included in all country weather reports, every major city has at least one street named after them and June 10 – Malvinas Day – is a national holiday.

The South Atlantic War

Until 1982, few people outside Argentina had ever heard about these controversial islands in the South Atlantic. Then suddenly they were splashed across all the newspapers around the world. On April 2, Argentine troops invaded these islands, easily ousted the token British force and claimed the islands as their own. The moment couldn't have been more opportune for General Leopoldo Galtieri, head of the military junta in control of the country at the time. Things had been going badly for him, but when he leant out of the balcony at Casa Rosada and told the jubilant masses below that Argentina was reclaiming what was rightfully theirs, the country's dire economic troubles and sinister 'disappearances' were momentarily forgotten. Only days before, thousands had taken to the streets to demonstrate against the junta; now they were clamouring their support.

Galtieri had found a solution – however temporary – to the trouble at home but he had underestimated the response of Margaret Thatcher's government. The junta believed the British would react with no more than a token protest. Instead they hastily gathered together a massive task force which steamed full ahead for the South Atlantic. The ensuing war was to last 72 days, claim over a thousand lives and cost $2 billion. Many of those killed were Argentines – more than 300 died when the Argentine cruiser *General Belgrano* was torpedoed and sunk outside the national exclusion zone. This particular incident causes much pain and anger even today. The Argentine forces wreaked their fair share of damage with their deadly Exocet missiles, sinking *HMS Sheffield* and other British ships but they were soon overwhelmed by the British forces and surrendered in Port Stanley on June 14. Over 10,000 Argentines were captured, many of them badly trained and poorly equipped young, often teenage, conscripts.

The military junta and the armed forces were thoroughly discredited by the defeat and Galtieri was booted out of office. Argentines were further outraged when they discovered that they had been fed misleading government propaganda that claimed Argentina had been winning the war. By the end of the debacle, the only group to come out with any respect was the Argentine air force, whose pilots' courage and personal bravery – their creed was death before dishonour – had been outstanding.

Meanwhile, the islands' status became more entrenched, with the 1,800 English-speaking islanders digging in their heels even further and refusing point-blank to ever accept Argentine sovereignty.

The Charm Offensive

Since the war, successive Argentine governments have sought to woo the islanders over to their way of thinking through a 'charm offensive'. President Menem had pledged that the islands would be Argentina's by the year 2000. The Argentine foreign minister sends the islanders gifts at Christmas, attends meetings and even sends them greeting cards on the Queen's birthday. But, as yet, all to no avail. Many of these gifts are returned unopened in an act of defiance; the rest, it's been said, are thrown onto minefields left by the Argentines during the war. In 1995, the Argentine foreign minister even offered to buy the islands, offering each 'kelper' an exorbitant sum of money to swap nationalities. However, the islanders remain adamant that they do not want anything to do with Argentina. The Malvinas will continue to be a thorn in the side of the foreign ministers on both sides of the Atlantic.

Don't Mention the War?

Tempers are still lost over the issue of island ownership and it's quite common to see graffiti around the country telling the English to 'get out' or declaring that the 'Malvinas were, are and always will be Argentine'. Occasionally this can escalate into something bigger. Following the war there were two attempts to blow up the *Torre de los Inglesas*, a 63 metre replica of Big Ben given to the people of Buenos Aires by the British in 1910 to celebrate Argentina's 100 years of independence. And on the eve of the 1986 Football World Cup quarter final clash between Argentina and England a headline in the populist *Crónica* newspaper screamed 'We're coming to get you, pirates!'

But where does this leave the British visitor to Argentina? From personal experience, providing you don't stick your neck out and go around saying that the islands are yours, it shouldn't be a problem. Being British myself, I had been hugely hesitant to bring the subject up in Argentina and was dreading the moment when someone – as was customary – would ask me where I was from and then turning out to

Photo: Jamie Grant

Memorial in Plaza de San Martín to those who fell in the 1982 South Atlantic War.

be an ex-*combatante*. Finally it happened, in a taxi tearing through Buenos Aires at the usual breakneck speed. My taxi driver, looking at me in the rear-view mirror with an enormous grin, told me how he had been only 19 years old at the time of the war and had been conscripted into the army the year before. He was captured after only 15 days and held prisoner on *HMS Canberra*, and by all accounts held absolutely no grudge against the English. 'The food on the ship was miles better than at home,' he told me. 'We were given pocket money and treated like gentlemen.' Then he casually changed the conversation. 'Hey, do you like the Beatles?'

Subsequent conversations with war veterans revealed that many held the opinion that the war had been a stupid and costly affair. No one I met appeared to have any serious antagonism towards British visitors. Sure, the Malvinas are indeed Argentine, they'd say, but let's forget all about the war.

Perhaps the most poignant epitaph on the war is from a poem, *Juan López and John Ward*, that Jorge Luis Borges wrote three years after the war, in 1985:

> 'They would have been friends, but they met only once
> face to face on some too famous islands, and each
> one was Cain and each one was Abel.
> They buried them together. Snow and corruption know
> them.
> The events to which I refer took place in a time that we
> cannot understand.'

Chapter Eight

LANGUAGE

At times, Argentines sound more Italian than Spanish. And like Italians and other Latin Americans, their sentences are accompanied by flamboyant hand and arm movements, wild gesticulations and lots of touching. You won't have to adopt such characteristics, but your efforts at speaking Spanish will be enormously appreciated. In fact, you won't be able to fade into the background in a conversation with the Argentines, who are an incredibly chatty and expressive people. You'll be drawn into conversations whether popping into the corner shop, waiting in a bank queue or squeezed in a bus. Just make sure you raise your voice so you can be heard above everyone else's clamour.

If you haven't mastered Spanish before you arrive in Argentina, you may well be surprised at how fast you'll pick it up thanks to all the practice you'll get once you start mingling with Argentines. Children, especially, tend to find it ridiculously easy, probably putting you to shame in the process.

If you do find that you are stumped for the right words, you won't have much trouble finding someone who speaks English, especially in the major cities, larger hotels and within business circles. And even if you are fluent in Spanish, most Argentines just won't be able to resist practising their English on you anyway. Many Argentines also speak, or at least understand, Italian, Portuguese, French and German.

But undoubtedly the best advice is to try and learn a few Spanish basics before you actually arrive in Argentina. This is not as daunting as it may seem. As far as foreign languages go, you couldn't have picked an easier one! The Spanish language is remarkably straight-forward and basically phonetic, with each letter consistently sounding like its name. A good pronunciation together with a foundation of vocabulary and grammar should mean that within a few weeks you'll be perfectly adept at ordering your *bife de chorizo* and holding your own in riotous conversation over a *mate* with your new Argentine friends. Even the shyest students of Spanish shouldn't hesitate to practise their newly acquired skills – you will be adored for doing so.

PRONUNCIATION

With most consonants pronounced almost exactly as they are in English, vowels play a crucial role in successful listening and speaking. Each of the five vowels never vary in pronunciation.

A is pronounced AH, like the *a* in father.
E is pronounced EH, like the first *e* in elephant.
I is pronounced as a shortened and sharp EE, like the *i* in tangerine.
O is pronounced as a short OH, like the *o* in dot.
U is pronounced like a shortened OO, like the *oo* in oops!

Only two Spanish consonant sounds do not exist in English: the *rr* which sounds like a trill (the tongue must flutter) and the *j*, as well as the *g* (when it comes before an *e* or an *i*), which sounds like someone clearing his throat, or like the *ch* in the Scottish *loch* or the German *ach*. A single *r* at the beginning of a word will also be rolled. Practise saying *que rapido ruedan las ruedas del ferrocarril*. If a native Spanish speaker can hear you say this without cringing, then you've mastered it.

There are some consonants that do not sound like their English counterparts:

H is silent.

Ñ is pronounced like the *ni* in onion.

QU is pronounced like the *k* in duck, with a silent *u*.

V is pronounced like a soft *b*. (To be clear with spellings, the Argentines will talk about *b larga* [tall b] or *v corta* [short v].)

Z is the same as *s*, with no buzzing or lisping sound as there is in Spain.

Most Argentines, but especially the *porteños* of Buenos Aires, pronounce the **y** and **ll** like the softened *zsh* sound found in the English words *measure* and *beige*. Thus *calle*, meaning 'street', would be pronounced *caishay* and *yo* (I) would be pronounced *zshoh*. In some parts of Argentina and most of the Spanish-speaking world, both the *ll* and the *y* are pronounced like the English *y* in yes.

Stress

Generally, if a letter in a word has an accent on it, then that letter should be pronounced with greater stress. If a word has no accent and ends in a vowel, or in *n* or *s*, then the second to last vowel is stressed. For words ending in a consonant other than *n* or *s*, the last syllable is stressed.

The Complicated Voseo

In addition to the giveaway accent and incredible slang (see below), in everyday Argentine Spanish, a telltale characteristic that distinguishes Argentines (and Uruguayans) from the rest of the Spanish-speaking world is their use of the grammatical form known as the *voseo*. In this form, the second person singular, *tu*, informal, meaning 'you', is substituted by the more stylised word *vos*. When the *voseo* is used, verbs will be conjugated slightly differently than in regular Spanish, usually taking on an extra accent. It is a shady topic that can throw even advanced students of Spanish. For example, *tu comes* (you eat) becomes *vos comés* in Argentina. In irregular verbs the difference is more striking. *Tu entiendes* (you understand) becomes *vos entendés*, *tu eres* (you are) becomes that giveaway Argentine expression *vos sos*. With no obvious pattern, these irregular verbs must be learnt individually. If you do get hopelessly confused, you can always resort to the original *tu* form which everyone understands, but this will immediately identify you as an outsider.

Throughout the Spanish-speaking world, the formal version of both *vos* and *tu* is *usted*, but in Latin America (including Argentina), the second person plural of both *tu* and *vos* is *ustedes* and never *vosotros* as it is in Spain.

KEY WORDS AND PHRASES

The following key words and phrases should provide you with a handful of very basic Spanish starters.

Greetings and Initial Meetings

Good morning	*Buenos días*
Good afternoon	*Buenas tardes*
Good evening/Goodnight	*Buenas noches*
Hello/hi	*Hola*
Pleased to meet you	*Encantado* (*encantada* for a woman)/*Mucho gusto*

How are you? (formal)	*Como esta usted?/Como le va?*
How's it going?/How are you? (informal)	*Como andas?/Como estas?*
Very well, thanks, and you?	*Muy bien gracias, y vos/usted?*
Please	*Por favor*
Thank you	*Gracias*
Thank you very much	*Muchas gracias*
You're welcome	*De nada/no hay porqué*
Goodbye	*Ciao/Adios*
See you later	*Nos vemos*
See you tomorrow	*Hasta mañana*
See you soon	*Hasta pronto*
Yes	*Sí*
No	*No*
I'm sorry	*Lo siento*
Excuse me	*Disculpe/Perdón*
I don't speak Spanish	*No hablo castellano*
Do you speak English?	*Habla usted ingles?*
I don't understand	*No entiendo*
Could you speak slower please	*Podría hablar más despacio, por favor*
What is your name? (formal)	*Como se llama usted?*
What is your name? (informal)	*Como te llamas?/Cual es tu nombre?*
Who shall I say is calling?	*De parte de quién?*
My name is John	*Me llamo John*
This is Maria	*Te presento Maria*
Where are you from? (formal)	*De donde es?*
Where do you come from? (informal)	*De donde sos?*
What do you do?	*A qué se dedica?*
Do you like Argentina?	*Le gusta Argentina?*
I love it	*Me encanta*

How do you say …?	*Como se dice …?*
How do you spell …?	*Como se escribe …?*
Don't bother me!	*No me molestes!*
Go away! (informal)	*Andate!*
Leave me alone, please	*Déjame en paz, por favor*

Shopping and Eating Out

Could I see the menu, please	*Puedo ver la carta, por favor*
I want	*Quiero*
I would like	*Quisiera*
Do you have …? (formal)	*Tiene …*
Do you have …? (informal)	*Tenés …?*
We would like to order, please	*Queremos pedir, por favor*
Would you like anything to drink?	*Algo para tomar?*
Let's make a toast	*Un brindis*
Cheers!/Bless you (after a sneeze)	*Salud!*
Bon appetit!	*Buen provecho!*
breakfast	*desayuno*
lunch	*almuerzo*
supper	*cena*
dessert	*postre*
I'm vegetarian	*Soy vegetariano*
The bill, please	*La cuenta, por favor*
Where can I buy …?	*Dónde puedo comprar …?*
Where can I find …?	*Dónde puedo encontrar …?*
How much does it cost?	*Cuánto cuesta?*
How much is it?	*Cuánto es?*
Do you have anything cheaper?	*Tiene algo más barato?*
Do you accept credit cards?	*Aceptan tarjetas de crédito?*
I'll take it	*Lo llevo*
Do you have this in my size?	*Tiene esto en mi talle?*
What size are you?	*Que talle es?*

I'm a 42	*Soy 42*
What shoe size do you take?	*Cuánto calzas?*
I take a 40 shoe size	*Calzo 40*
Give me a kilo of ... please	*Deme un kilo de ... por favor*
a pound	*una libra*
a litre	*un litro*
a metre	*un metro*

Directions and Travel

Where is ...?	*Dónde esta/queda ...?*
How do I get to Córdoba?	*Como puede llegar a Córdoba?*
On the right/left	*a la derecha/izquerida*
straight on	*derecho*
up	*arriba*
down	*abajo*
one block	*una cuadra/manzana*
the bathroom/toilet	*el baño*
the tourist office	*la oficina de turismo*
the post office	*el correo*
the bank	*el banco*
the hospital	*la hospital*
the embassy	*la embajada*
the main square	*la plaza principal*
the train station	*la estación de ferrocarril*
the bus stop	*la parada*
the airport	*el aeropuerto*
aeroplane	*avión*
bus terminal	*terminal de buses*
the bus	*el colectivo*
the subway	*el subte*
ticket	*boleto*
return ticket	*boleto ida y vuelta*
When does the next plane/train/bus for ... leave?	*Cuando sale el próximo avión/ tren/colectivo para ...?*

Do you have a room?	*Tiene un cuarto?*
For one/for two	*para uno/para dos*
With a private bathroom	*con baño privado*
With air-conditioning/heating	*con aire condicionado/ calefacción*
Is breakfast included?	*Esta incluido el desayuno?*

Telling the Time

What time is it?	*Qué hora es?*
Could you tell me the time please?	*Podría decirme la hora por favor?*
It's eight o'clock	*Son las ocho*
It's eight forty-five	*Son las nueve menos cuarto* (literally nine minus a quarter)
It's five thirty	*Son las cinco y media*
It's one o'clock	*Es la una*
In the morning	*por la mañana*
At night	*de la noche*
Today	*hoy*
Yesterday	*ayer*
Tomorrow	*mañana*
Early	*temprano*
Late	*tarde*

Numbers

1	*uno*
2	*dos*
3	*tres*
4	*cuatro*
5	*cinco*
6	*seis*
7	*siete*
8	*ocho*
9	*nueve*

10	*diez*
11	*once*
12	*doce*
13	*trece*
14	*catorce*
15	*quince*
16	*dieciseis*
17	*diecisiete*
18	*dieciocho*
19	*diecinueve*
20	*veinte*
21	*veintiuno*
22	*veintidos*
30	*treinta*
40	*cuarenta*
50	*cincuenta*
60	*sesenta*
70	*setenta*
80	*ochenta*
90	*noventa*
100	*cien*
200	*doscientos*
300	*trescientos*
1000	*mil*
1,000,000	*un millon*

Days of the Week

Monday	*lunes*
Tuesday	*martes*
Wednesday	*miércoles*
Thursday	*jueves*
Friday	*viernes*
Saturday	*sábado*
Sunday	*domingo*

Months of the Year

January	*enero*
February	*febrero*
March	*marzo*
April	*abril*
May	*mayo*
June	*junio*
July	*julio*
August	*agosto*
September	*septiembre*
October	*octubre*
November	*noviembre*
December	*deciembre*

PUTTING YOUR FOOT IN YOUR MOUTH

If you learnt your Spanish in Spain or in another Latin American country, take care. Argentines have invented new words and twisted all sorts of other words around. The most obvious potential *faux pas* is the word *coger* which for most Spanish speakers means 'to take' as in 'to take a bus'. In Argentina, however, *coger* means 'to have sex with someone'. In Buenos Aires, one would never *coge un colectivo*!

It is also worth noting that *facturas* are not only a bunch of bills and invoices as they would be in other Spanish-speaking countries, but can also mean something altogether much more delicious – an assortment of pastries, usually stuffed with sticky *dulce de leche* caramel, that go down a treat with a *café cortado* at teatime.

Beware, also, of the following false friends that English-speaking Spanish students must contend with: *preservativos* are condoms and not jam. If you are *embarazada*, you are pregnant and not embarrassed, while *nafta* in Argentina means gasoline and not the trade agreement.

SLANG

The use of slang in everyday speech is so extensive and widespread that Argentina could at times almost boast its own language.

As waves of immigrants from around the globe poured into the port of Buenos Aires, they brought with them their own languages, and many of their words stuck and are still used today. Since most of the immigrants came from Italy and Spain, what emerged as the local slang is derived from a ferociously fast blend of Spanish and Italian – a colourful and unique fusion known as *lunfardo*. Unless you've grown up speaking both Italian and Spanish at home, *lunfardo* is up there on the incomprehensibility stakes with London's rhyming cockney slang.

You will hear *lunfardo* spoken throughout the country, but its epicentre is Buenos Aires, where it was born in the brothels and city tenements at the turn of the century. Just a quick skip across the pages of a *lunfardo* dictionary and it becomes crystal clear that this was once the language of crooks, drunks, brothel customers, thieves, the down-and-out and the brokenhearted. (*Lunfardo* comes into its own when used in the lyrics of the tango.)

If you think you're confused now, *lunfardo* gets even stranger. In its most warped extreme it switches the last syllable of the word with the first syllable. Thus *café* becomes *feca*, *mujer* becomes *jermu*, *vino* becomes *novi*, and the *tango* becomes the *gotan*.

Try and get your hands on a copy of José Gobello's *Nuevo Diccionario Lunfardo* if you can.

'Argentinianisms'

The following words are used in everyday Argentine speech, and probably won't mean anything to you if you learnt to speak Spanish outside Argentina. Many of the words are unadulterated *lunfardo* and some are straightforward slang evolved over the years. Argentines also use the normal Spanish equivalent. (Wherever possible, the corresponding Spanish word is given in italics within parentheses.)

181

alucinante	amazing/incredible (*increíble*)
atacado	hassled/stressed (*estresado*)
bache	pothole in the road; you'll come across a lot of these
bárbaro	cool, great, fantastic (*estupendo/magnifico*)
barra brava	organised group of football hooligans, usually armed and looking for a fight
birra	beer (*cerveza*)
bocha	a lot (*montón*)
boliche	nightclub/disco (*club/discoteca*)
bolita	a Bolivian, derogatory (*boliviano*)
boludez	a stupid thing (*tontería*)
boludo/a	(literally big-balled), means something like twat or asshole; affectionate or aggressive form of address, depending on tone of voice
bondi	bus (*bus/autobus*)
bostero	Boca Juniors football club fan
brazuca	a Brazilian (*brasileño*)
bronca	fury/anger – to be mad at something or someone (*rabia*)
buchón	sneak/gossipmonger (*soplón/chismoso*)
cana	prison or the police, literally a grey hair (*cárcel/policia*)
canchero	show-off, a cool guy who knows it
catrera	a bed, especially one for frolicking (*cama*)
chabón	man, guy or bloke (*hombre*)
chancho	ticket collector, derogatory (*guarda*)
chanta	slightly sleazy charmer, greaser, fraud, chancer
che	friend, mate, hey you (a common form of address)
china	girl or woman, men may talk about *mi china* (my woman), especially popular in the countryside where it is an old-fashioned name for a gaucho's girl (*chica/mujer*)
chorro	thief (*ladrón*)

coco	head, literally a coconut (*cabeza*)
colectivo	bus, also known as *bondi* (*bus/autobus*)
encurdelarse	to get drunk, inebriated (*emborracharse*)
farándula	Argentina's jet set of models, TV stars, actors and polo players
faso	cigarette, usually a marijuana joint
fiaca	bone idle, lazy, lethargic; if you have *fiaca*, you can't be bothered to do anything (*pereza*)
fifi	fashion-conscious man, dandy
flash	something cool/great
forro	condom or scumbag, vulgar (*condón*)
gallego	a Spaniard, due to the fact that many Spanish immigrants came from Galicia (*español*)
gallina	River Plate football club fan
gardeliano	fan of tango singer Carlos Gardel
gauchada	a favour, a spontaneous act of generosity
gaucho	the original Argentine cowboy, now used to describe a ranch hand or man from the countryside
guacho	literally a stray but used as an insult, like 'bastard' (not to be confused with *gaucho*)
guita	money, cash (*plata/dinero*)
joya	great/good (*bueno*)
laburante	worker (*trabajador*)
laburar	to work (*trabajar*); work itself is *laburo* (*trabajo*)
loco	bloke/guy (literally a mad one)
luco	a thousand pesos
macana	terrible, as in *Qué macana!* What a shame!
macanudo	great, fantastic person, a good sport (*buen tipo*)
mango	a peso; if something costs 5 mangos, it costs 5 pesos
milicos	the military (*militares*)
mina	girl – in tango lyrics it describes a gangster's moll, now for all young women (*chica/mujer*)
morfar	to eat (*comer*)

nafta	petrol/gas (*gasolina*)
ñoqui	a potato pasta traditionally eaten on the 29th of each month; also a public employee who shows up only on pay day
pajuerano	country bumpkin, yokel
papa	a beautiful thing of top quality or use
papelón	embarrassing thing or situation (*cosa vergonzosa*)
paraguas	a Paraguayan, derogatory (*paraguayo*)
pedo	drunk (literally a fart), as in *estoy en pedo/tenia un pedo* – I am drunk/I was so drunk (*borracho*). If you are *al pedo*, however, it means you're not doing anything (*a la deriva*).
pelotas	balls, usually used in the sense of *no me rompes las pelotas* – don't break my balls!
pelotudo	same as *boludo*
pendejo	insult, meaning a fool, stupid (literally pubic hair)
pibe/a	guy, kid (*chico/chica*)
pingos	the horses (at a race)
piola	used to describe something that is cool or trendy or someone who is cunning and astute
porteño	inhabitant of Buenos Aires, 'from the port'
potro	a cute guy
pucho	cigarette (*cigarillo*)
re	a prefix that means 'really' or 'very', as in *re-frio esta* – it's really cold
seco	dry/without money
tacho	taxi; a taxi driver may be referred to as a *tachero* (*taxi*)
tano	an Italian (*italiano*)
telo	hotel with rooms rented out on an hourly basis, also known as an *albergue transitorio*
trasnochador	someone who stays up all night, commonly encountered in Argentina

trucho	bogus, fake, something that is not what it appears to be (*falso*)
turco	a generalisation to describe a Muslim or a member of the Syrian community in Buenos Aires
quilombo	a mess or a brawl (*lío*)
viejos	parents (*padres*)
villa miseria	a shantytown
viveza criolla	native cunning or artful lying, carried out by a *vivo*
vivo	someone on the ball, quick to react to a given situation; a typical *porteño*

Useful Insults

Insider knowledge of key insults will prove invaluable, especially if you decide to take to the road. Insults range from quite light-hearted jests to the rather more offensive. In a nation where the family is considered practically sacred, an insult on the female members (both mothers and sisters) is especially damning. The most commonly used offensive expression is *hijo de puta*, the equivalent of 'you son of a bitch'. If that is too extreme, you can always fall back on punchy little words such as *pelado* (baldy) or *gordo* (fatty). Spoken in the right tone, they can be quite offensive, especially if followed by the suffix *de mierda* (literally 'shitty').

Another popular Argentine insult is *boludo*, literally 'big-balled'. Said sweetly, this form of address can be quite affectionate and is commonly used between friends. Said in an angry tone, however, it can suddenly become remarkably abusive.

Unless you are superconfident speaking Spanish, don't jump in straight away with all these 'Argentinianisms' or insults. You could end up making a fool of yourself, or worse still, cause unintentional offence by using them in unsuitable circumstances.

BODY LANGUAGE

Like most other Latin Americans, Argentines are very touchy-feely during conversations and their concept of personal space is vastly diminished in relation to the North American or North European norm. Don't jump back or try to edge away when an Argentine is hovering a matter of millimetres from your nose. Just as you shouldn't flinch if they grab your arm to emphasise a particularly important point or decide to casually pick lint off your suit.

Argentine men gathered together may appear to be acting in a way that doesn't seem awfully macho to an outsider. They will happily stroll down the street with their arms round each other and embrace and kiss old friends affectionately. At football matches don't be surprised to see grown men hug and kiss each other or burst into tears.

As you learn to speak Argentine Spanish, you will soon discover that most sentences are usually backed up with an incredible amount of hand and arm movements. I have known quite reserved foreigners who, like most of us, normally speak keeping their hands and arms perfectly immobile. But as soon as they start to learn Argentine Spanish, they automatically start to use amazing gesticulations. Then, when they revert to speaking their native tongue again, they cease flapping their arms about. It happens to me all the time.

As difficult as it is to resist, don't be too eager to jump in with wild gesticulations until you have ascertained their true meaning. Certain gestures that are perfectly harmless where you come from could send out unintentional messages or even cause great offence in Argentina. A selection of the most common gesticulations are listed below:

- A hand, palm down, stroking the underside of your chin away from the body means either a dismissive 'I don't know' or 'I don't care'.
- An outstretched arm with hand, palm down, making a scratching motion means 'come here'.
- A hand held palm up, with fingertips bunched together jabbing up into the air, means 'what's up?' 'what's going on?' or 'what's your

problem?' A flashier variation involving both hands making the gesture is generally employed in times of great exasperation.

- A hand holding an imaginary pen in the air making short squiggles is a wonderfully easy way of asking for the check/bill in a crowded restaurant or café. The movement is usually accompanied by mouthing the words, *La cuenta, por favor*.
- Slapping the back of one hand into the open palm of the other is a sign for money that could mean 'he earns a lot', 'it costs a lot' or 'pay up, buddy'.
- The index finger gently pulling down the outer corner of the eye warns 'watch out,' 'keep an eye out on that guy' or 'I know what you're up to'.

It's also a good idea to watch your facial movements during card games. *Truco*, in particular, involves an incredible amount of facial expressions to aid cheating. It's all very confusing so at the card table at least it's best to keep a poker face at all times.

PIROPOS

As you walk through the streets of Argentina, don't be surprised to hear men murmuring suggestive comments to passing women. What you are hearing are known as *piropos* and such behaviour is considered perfectly normal.

In the good old days catcalls or *piropos* always used to be snatches of poetry and romantic compliments. In modern times, *piropos* can still be lovely and eloquent gestures. However, occasionally they may also be slightly vulgar or involve inappropriate requests. Like chat-up lines in bars, women must ignore them and are never expected to respond or take the man up on his offer.

But *piropos* are not always that easy to ignore. As you (a woman) walk down the street, a man approaching from the opposite direction might well stop dead in his tracks, fling his arms wide open and blatantly eye you up and down. Then, once he's sure he's caught your eye, he will say something like 'Darling, if beauty were a sin, then you'd be unforgivable!' or 'Oh my God, I didn't know that flowers could walk.' I have seen grown women break out into giggles when this happens. Don't worry if you can't help but smile at the *piropo*; the man, needless to say, will be ecstatic. Of course, if a truly lovely compliment comes your way, a smile or a simple 'thank you' is entirely acceptable.

HOT TOPICS TO TALK ABOUT

Argentines love to chat so don't worry about any awkward silences on your part; they will go unnoticed in the incessant background noise. You will soon discover that Argentines are quite capable of talking about anything for hours on end, ranging from mundane waffle to intense debates on the meaning of life.

Social customs in Argentina are all geared towards conversation. The whole art of the *asado* (barbecue) as well as the *mate* ritual provide the perfect excuse for a good chinwag. For this reason alone, you should never turn down an invitation to drink *mate* or eat beef.

If you do come unstuck, which is enormously unlikely, here are some key conversation pointers:

Football: Given the country's obsession with football (soccer to North Americans), this is naturally a great starting point. Just make sure you know your Maradona from your Pele or you risk making a fool of yourself. Everyone in Argentina – young, old, male and female – has a fair grasp of the basics of the game just as everyone also has an opinion and a team that they back until death. To swap teams or allegiances is abominable, so don't suddenly become a Boca Juniors fan just because it seems everybody else is. I once observed a middle-aged German man from Frankfurt who couldn't speak a word of Spanish having the most animated conversation with a teenager from Salta who couldn't speak a word of German. Only a discussion on the World Cup would allow this. Learn some phrases such as *De que* *cuadro sos?* or *De que equipo sos?* (Which football team do you support?) and just see the glint light up in their eyes!

Family: This is another great topic of interest in Argentina where everyone is considered fair game for probing inquiries into their private lives and marital status. Whether you are married, have children or are thinking about getting married are all standard questions that you'll be expected to answer on spec.

Fashion: You can't go wrong on this subject. Argentines are incredibly fashion-conscious and will love to know about any of the latest fashions from your neck of the woods. If you want to see just how easy it is to break the ice, try saying something like 'What a lovely skirt. Where did you get it from?' (*Que linda pollera, donde la compraste?*)

Politics and the Economy: Argentines, in general, tend to be very well informed on current political and economic affairs and enjoy discussing them in great detail. Many Argentines will be quite happy to tell you who they voted for in the last election, and why, and will have strong opinions on the day's news and issues.

Discussions on politics and the economy can get quite heated, especially if you get onto the subjects of corruption, *peronismo* and how nothing ever works. It's amazing how a common gripe can unite people. Complaining about queues, things that don't work, power cuts and broken elevators or even the lousy weather can also prove to be a real bonding experience.

Argentines may frequently knock their own country, but don't be as enthusiastic on the subject yourself, at least with initial acquaintances. This also applies to the more sensitive subjects, such as the issue of ownership of disputed territories.

Culture: Argentines love going out to cinemas and theatres, and make very demanding audiences, so this will provide endless material for discussions on the latest film or show.

Because of their varied immigrant backgrounds and the fact that many Argentines themselves love to travel abroad, you will find yourself drawn into conversations on different cultures and countries around the world. In fact, just being foreign will give you an immediate advantage in the conversation stakes. Everyone will be desperate to know all about your home culture and how Argentina compares with it. Your positive comments about Argentina and its people will be hugely relished.

NAMES AND SURNAMES

When addressing people in Argentina it is worth noting that the Argentines generally tend to follow North American rules rather than the Latin American or Spanish norm for surnames. This makes things a lot more straightforward when addressing people formally or being addressed yourself as it involves just one surname. For example, if Maria Lopez marries Juan Sanchez, she will be known as Maria Sanchez. (In Mexico and other Latin countries, on the other hand, she would be known as Maria Lopez de Sanchez.) Meanwhile Juan and Maria's child – Juanito – will take just his father's surname: Juanito Sanchez. (The more traditional Latin American and Spanish custom combines both the father's surname with the mother's maiden surname, giving the child the name Juanito Sanchez Lopez.)

Argentines may well revert to the traditional Spanish custom of using two surnames on official documents, driving licences, passports and even in the phone book, especially if the surname is a common one and could be confused with others. Do remember, however, that this being Argentina, with its colourful multicultural background, there are bound to be exceptions to the rule. So remain fairly open-minded on the subject, and if in doubt play it safe with a simple *Señor* or *Señora*.

— Chapter Nine —

SURVIVAL SKILLS

'Mad dogs and Englishmen go out in the midday sun. …
Argentines sleep firmly from twelve to one …'

—Noel Coward in *Mad Dogs and Englishmen*

Argentina isn't the sort of country where things are going to run
without a hitch. This, undoubtedly, is part of its appeal. Still, you
can never know enough of those unwritten rules or have sufficient
insider knowledge essential for a happy survival.

In the worst case scenario, you're going to find yourself up against enormous quantities of *viveza criolla*, a bureaucratic minefield or some of the most terrifying driving on earth. But do remember that however bogged down or lost you get, in Argentina at least, there is always someone happy to help you out. The following no frills guide should prove indispensable for those planning on setting up and settling down in Argentina.

PLANES, TRAINS AND AUTOMOBILES

Driving in Argentina falls into a category somewhere between Mad Max and the Grand Prix. Drivers are happy to tackle any type of road, however dreadful, in whatever weather, but generally at some speed. In the cities, particularly in Buenos Aires, driving is exceptionally aggressive. If speed has to be cut because of rush hour congestion, the *porteño* driver will make up for lost time with vigorous lane hopping, honking, swerving out of the way of oncoming traffic at the last minute and taking corners on two wheels. Needless to say, there are frequent prangs accompanied by much shouting, exchanges of offensive hand signs and amazing strings of verbal abuse at other drivers (see Chapter 8). Often, after an accident, drivers get out onto the street to settle the argument as to who was the worse driver or whose fault it was, much to the amusement and delight of other motorists.

Buses

Bus drivers are widely respected and, of course, macho. In many rural areas buses are the only means of regular transport and the drivers may also act as postmen, paper boys and bread deliverers rolled in one. Argentina's major cities are connected by good bus links and the regional service is extensive, reaching smaller towns and villages. On long-distance bus services there is usually air-conditioning and toilets on board. Prices are competitive, because many companies run the same routes.

City buses or *colectivos* are an institution in their own right, hurtling through the congested traffic at breakneck speed with passengers packed like sardines and clinging on for dear life around corners. Make sure you board with enough small change – banknotes won't do – to feed into the metallic machine that will spit out your ticket. Bus trips usually cost 70 centavos within the city centre and slightly more for trips to the suburbs. Hang on to your ticket for the duration of the journey in case of a spot check.

You should always board the bus at the driver's end and alight at the rear. But be quick at both ends as the *colectivo* won't hang around. *Colectivo* drivers run on a tight schedule and can be understandably gruff, irritated by inspectors constantly breathing down their necks.

There are hundreds of different set bus routes in Buenos Aires and other large cities and the buses that run along them are all numbered. If you're lost, just ask any local, or better still, inquire at a nearby kiosk, about the best bus route to get where you want to go, and they'll point you to the appropriate *parada* (bus stop). It may also be worth getting your hands on a bus guide (see the Strategic Directory, Chapter 10). Strangely enough, queues at bus stops are some of the most orderly in Argentina and are not usually barged.

Taxis

Unless you're a diehard adrenaline junkie, never ask your cabbie to step on it. Never ask them to slow down either – they could get quite offended. In Buenos Aires, with almost 40,000 cabs on the streets, it's easy to get a lift on any street at any time except when it's raining; *porteños* don't like getting wet. But with one cab for every 83 people in Buenos Aires – compared to, say, New York where there is one taxi for every 295, or London, with one for every 505 – you're never going to have to wait too long. Taxis are black with a yellow roof and the flag-down fare is just over a dollar, rising steadily every 250 metres. Taxi rates are relatively good and cheap in Argentina – a ten-minute journey across downtown Buenos Aires should cost just US$5.

It is rare to find a taxi driver – or *tachero* as they are known in the local slang – lost for words. As in all countries throughout the world, but probably even more so in Argentina, your taxi driver will be a source of unbelievable amounts of local information. If anyone knows what's going on in town and why, it will be him (female taxi drivers are few and far between). Don't be afraid to strike up a conversation; they certainly won't.

For longer trips, such as to the airport, it may be best to employ the services of a *remise*. This is a private car with a driver that can be hired out for the day, a week or one long trip. For long journeys, they will generally be cheaper than taxis and prices are negotiable beforehand – but they don't drive any slower!

Most taxis are genuine but there are reports of occasional bogus drivers. Make sure the taxi you get into has a meter and a driver's ID hanging from the back seat. It is also recommended to flag down a moving taxi rather than one waiting on the curb, in case it's a set-up.

Car Hire and Buying

If you are planning an extended stay, you may well consider hiring or even buying a vehicle. All the leading international car hire companies, including Hertz, Localiza and Budget, are represented in Argentina. Prices are relatively high, anything from US$75 to $145 per day. You must also be at least 21 and have a valid international driver's licence to supplement your local driver's licence. (Some agencies may require the hirer to be at least 25 years old.)

You probably won't be able to pick up a good second-hand car for less than US$4,000 in Argentina. Popular models are Peugeot, Ford, Fiat and Renault. Do make sure you have the title to the car (known as a *tarjeta verde* or green card) and that your licence tax payments are up to date. It must also be fully insured (the more expensive the car, the more the insurance, but it should cost around US$220 per year). Foreigners will also need authorised permission to take a car bought in Argentina out of the country.

Once you know the sign, spotting a second-hand car for sale is easy. Argentines have invented an ingenious alternative to the straightforward 'For Sale' sign stuck on the windscreen. And although a sign may be put up, the more usual form is to stand an empty bottle on the roof of the proffered car (naturally, when parked). If the car interests you, simply inquire at the nearest household.

Driving Tips

Numerous surveys have identified Argentina as having the highest number of road deaths. On average 8,000 people die each year on Argentina's roads – that's about one death every hour. Car accidents are the main cause of death among young Argentines and crashes periodically knock off Argentina's rich and famous.

It's not surprising then that all motorists are required by law to wear a seatbelt, carry a first-aid kit, a rigid tow bar, two warning triangles and a fire extinguisher. Few do. Transport laws in Argentina, like red lights, were made to be skipped.

If you do decide to take the plunge, drive on the right, brace yourself for a complicated system of one-way streets in cities and never back down in an argument with other motorists ... it's simply not macho!

On national and provincial roads you will come across occasional police checkpoints, where drivers frantically reach to put on seatbelts, only to remove them again as soon as they are out of sight. If you are stopped by the transport police it is important that you can show your driver's licence, the green card (which proves your car is registered with the local council) and up-to-date insurance papers. If you fail to produce any of these on spec, you could face a heavy fine or, more commonly, be asked for a bribe.

Make sure you always travel with plenty of change as most roads have tollgates on them. The trip from Buenos Aires to Mar del Plata, for example, will cost you about US$12, passing through all the tollgates.

Typical traffic and pedestrian chaos in Buenos Aires.

Driving Licence

If you already have a driving licence from your home country, before you leave get an international driver's licence, which, in conjunction with your original licence, is valid throughout Argentina.

To be eligible for an Argentine driving licence, you must be at least 17 years old. You must pay a fee of US$100 at the municipal offices, and will be required to pass an eyesight test as well as a short and fairly easy driving test in an enclosed area. There are no compulsory lessons and no written exams. The licence is valid for five years, after which you must reapply.

Parking

Many cars have reinforced bumpers for the purpose of getting a large object into a very small parking space. On level ground it is unwise to leave your handbrake on. With this sort of parking going on, your car – if handbraked – will mount the neighbouring car, rather than just move along in a queue of pushed cars. Of course, it is inadvisable to park near a corner – you could get pushed out into the stream of traffic. In short, it is not unusual to find your car in a different place from where you left it.

Pedestrians

In Argentina, near-suicidal driving takes place on roads that are in a constant state of chaos and ongoing repair. Like the streets, pavements are riddled with holes ranging in size from small potholes to what could pass for mine shafts. Loose paving stones wobble and trip you up and shoot a jet of water up your leg as you step onto them. At the same time, the pedestrian is required to keep an eye out for water from air-conditioning outlets and dehumidifiers dripping from above. Surprisingly few locals come to grief. Argentines seem to have inbuilt radars for avoiding these obstacles while carrying on animated conversations, with frequent unexpected stops in mid-pavement to emphasise a point. Pedestrian traffic is much like road traffic – unpredictable and erratic.

As if all this wasn't bad enough, Buenos Aires also lays claim to arguably the 'world's widest road'. At its widest – some 20 lanes – the *Avenida Nueve de Julio* is every pedestrian's nightmare, but there's no avoiding it as it literally divides the city in two. Sooner or later any visitor to Buenos Aires has to take the plunge and cross it. The city council eventually took pity on the elderly and constructed concrete resting benches halfway across next to small blue signs that warn pedestrians to 'Avoid Accidents, Don't Run.' Who are they kidding? When the lights change to green and you're only halfway across with several tons of cold steel bearing down on you at top speed, do what everyone else does. *Run!*

And a final word of warning. Just when you think you're out of danger, a motorbike will whizz through a stream of stationary cars and mount the pavement. The rider may want to chat to a group of friends, deliver a pizza or just park, while giving you – the pedestrian

197

– a mild coronary in the process. Motorbike helmets are simply a technicality; they are usually pushed up back off the forehead, adding an even more dashing dimension to these kamikaze riders. Bicycle helmets are unheard of.

Hitchhiking

Friends who have hitchhiked swear that it's the best way to get to know the country, provided you're patient and have plenty of time on your hands. Hitchhiking is relatively difficult in Argentina, but this hasn't stopped people from trying. Most trucking companies prohibit their drivers from giving lifts and even private car owners are wary since a highly publicised case of a hitchhiker suing the driver of the car he was travelling in after it crashed. Your best bet is to hang out at a gas station, or walk along the roadside and look hopeful. It's also a good idea to look clean and respectable.

Have a back-up plan (such as a tent and extra rations of food and water) in case you find yourself stuck in the middle of nowhere. Better still, try and make sure that you're always dropped off within walking distance of a town as you may get stranded for days – especially in Patagonia.

Remember that you are taking a risk when you hitchhike anywhere in the world.

Driving in Patagonia

Driving in Patagonia deserves a special mention purely because it couldn't be more different than anything you've done before. Argentine road veteran Dan Buck, who has regularly braved the Patagonian roads while doing research on Patagonia's famous outlaws Butch and Sundance, sums it up:

'Three animal species plague motorists in Patagonia: sheep, hares, and night drivers.

'Sheep are cute, fluffy, but maddening. Whatever direction a sheep is running, at the last second it'll run the opposite.

Photo: Jamie Grant

Don't attempt to cross this Patagonian bridge by car!

Bounding along the roadside, angling away from your car, a sheep will pivot in front of you right when it's too late to hit the brakes. Whomp! Perversely, if the sheep is on a collision course with your left fender, just before impact it will execute an about-face. This is a guaranteed fact of nature.

'Hares, on the other hand, will do exactly what they'll look like they'll do. Leap out onto the road. Squish. Fortunately the *liebres*, as they are known locally, are multitudinous. They number in the tens of thousands, maybe millions (they won't sit down long enough to be counted). The dozens you flatten won't be missed.

'Night drivers, however, will unnerve even the most experienced on-the-road motorist. Night drivers in Patagonia use only one set of lights – high beams. There is nothing as harrowing as Ruta 40 on a moonless, coal-black night. Sheep

zig and zag, hares dart through the air like so many furry
locusts, and head-on round a dusty curve comes a pair of
dazzling rockets of incandescent light that send you into a
spasm of blindness, off the road, and into a ditch.'

Aeroplanes

Argentina has several domestic airlines: Aerolineas Argentinas,
Austral, LAPA, DINAR and LAER. Prices can be high, but Argentina's vast distances often make this the most viable option for
traversing the country. With some flights, if you book in advance, you
can get a much cheaper fare, so always ask if there are any promotions
or discounts going. There are also the regional airlines: Kaiken,
Andesmar, Southern Winds and LADE, the army airline. These
specialise in different regions and may be more economical, so
always shop around for the best ticket.

For those planning on an intensive flying visit to Argentina, it
may be worthwhile buying a *Visit Argentina* ticket. Costing about
US$450, it gives you four flight coupons (additional coupons cost
US$120 a go) that can be used on any Aerolineas Argentinas or
Austral flight within the country. Sounds great, but here's the catch.
The four flights must all be taken within one month. Furthermore, the
ticket has to be bought outside Argentina in conjunction with an

international flight ticket. One flight counts as a coupon even if you are taking an immediate connection, which is quite likely considering that most trips between provincial cities have to fly via Buenos Aires. To travel from Mendoza to Salta, for example, will use up two flight coupons as the route takes you via Buenos Aires where you have to get a connection. Finally, you must plan the entire route in advance since only one change is free of charge; it costs US$50 for every other change. So, great for those who know exactly what they want, when they want it. Not so great for the spontaneous types or those likely to change their minds.

Most international flights to and from Argentina arrive at Ezeiza airport, 45 kilometres from downtown Buenos Aires. Taxis and *remises* take you downtown for US$30–40 and a bus service run by Manuel Tienda León takes you there or back for about US$15. There is an airport departure tax of US$16 for international flights and US$13 for flights to neighbouring South American countries. Domestic flights and those to Uruguay leave from downtown Buenos Aires at Jorge Newbery airport; the departure tax is US$3 for domestic flights and US$5 for flights to Uruguay. Airport taxes can be paid in pesos or dollars and may be included in the ticket price.

Trains

Argentina's once magnificent railway system has disintegrated over the years, receiving its final deathblow during the privatisation programme of the 1990s. Only a fraction of the main train services still run, and most of these go very slowly indeed, allowing passengers ample opportunity to admire the scenery.

Most of Argentina's railways were built by the British and were British-owned until they were nationalised under Perón in the 1940s. Many of the railway terminals, such as Retiro and Constitucion, hark back to Victorian Britain. The trains themselves are quite old-fashioned. There are also, however, more modern electric trains that connect downtown Buenos Aires with its suburbs.

Photo: Jamie Grant

Majestic Retiro station, with a British twist.

Not only those wishing to travel will board the trains as they pull out of stations. A swarm of street vendors, selling everything from biros to bibles, wade through the passengers depositing goods for sale on their laps, then wade back again collecting the money. If you don't want to buy the bible/biro/shaving kit/set of felt-tip pens, show no interest and they will eventually be removed from your lap.

For railway buffs, Argentina boasts its own 'great train journeys'. One particularly arresting track known as the *Tren a las Nubes* (Train to the Clouds) is internationally renowned. Running from the city of Salta to the Chilean frontier, it is literally breathtaking when it reaches heights of over 4,000 metres and, at one stage, crosses *La Polvorilla*, an awesome iron viaduct. In true South American laid-back style, construction took almost 30 years, and by the time it opened in 1948 it wasn't of much use any more thanks to advances in air and road technology. Nowadays, the train runs mainly for tourists.

Other great train journeys include the 27-hour slog from Tucumán to Buenos Aires (if you want comfort, legroom and air-conditioning, travel Pullman class). The six-hour train journey from Buenos Aires to Mar del Plata provides a much safer option than the 400 kilometre Route 2, alarmingly dubbed by local motorists 'the death route'. There is even a working railway in Tierra de Fuego (built by convicts) that can claim to be the southernmost train journey in the world.

Train travel also has its pitfalls. An increasingly irksome national pastime appears to be throwing stones at passing trains. These hit the window with an enormous crack and if the angle and force are just right, the glass smashes.

'Who is doing this?' I asked my neighbour, Alfonso, on a train somewhere between Tucumán and Buenos Aires, after a rock crashed off our windowpane in the buffet car at eye level.

'It's bored kids mainly,' he told me, quite unperturbed. 'But grown-ups throw stuff as well, especially if there's been a football match.'

'Does anyone ever get hurt?'

'Oh yes,' he replied, quite animated. 'I've often seen people bleeding in their seats.'

We felt like sitting ducks, especially as the train crawled at a snail's pace through towns and villages, when even the most innocent child raising his hand to wave left passengers cringing in their seats. Still, you can't beat train travel for romance and history. Chugging into Buenos Aires on a warm summer's evening, you can imagine you're 15-year-old Evita, running away with a tango singer.

El Subte

Buenos Aires' underground metro system, known as *el subte*, was built in 1913 with five main lines, four of which (A, B, D and E) run almost parallel to each other from downtown Buenos Aires to the northern and western suburbs. Only one line (Linea C) crosses them, connecting the major train stations of Constitucion and Retiro. Some *subte* carriages are wonderfully old and rattling affairs with wooden panels and gilded mirrors – although the doors don't necessarily always close before the train moves off. Many trains, however, have had their old carriages exchanged for more modern ones.

Providing they run in the direction you want to go, this is a fast and cheap option for traversing the city. Fares are just 60 cents a trip (including changes, provided you stay underground). Buy up a bunch of tokens (*fichas*) in advance as this will save you having to queue at the ticket office every time you want to travel. You should also make sure you pass through the correct turnstile to the platform going in your direction or else you will have to leave and use another *ficha*.

Subte maps are available free of charge from *subte* ticket offices.

ACCOMMODATION

Accommodation in Argentina caters for every taste. There are sparkling new apartments fashioned after Miami for the modernists out there; then again you might be seduced by an enchanting tiled courtyard or an overgrown balcony in a turn-of-the-century building. If you choose an older building, brace yourself for a series of Heath Robinson-like contraptions held together with sticky tape, unravelled paper clips and a terrifying system of exposed wiring. (The toilet in my apartment had to be flushed with an old telephone cable.) But whatever its state, the Argentine's house is his castle and great pride is taken in keeping it clean and gleaming.

Hotels

These range from luxurious five-star hotels such as the grandiose Alvear Palace Hotel in Buenos Aires to raucous hostels filled with a young international crowd of backpackers squeezed into bunk beds and sharing a communal kitchen. For the latter, try and get hold of an International Youth Hostel Card or an International Student Identity Card before you arrive and be sure to flash it and ask for a discount as you check in. Argentines themselves love to travel, so whatever type of hotel you choose to stay in, you will almost certainly mingle just as much with Argentines as with other foreigners.

A youth hostel may be known as a *hostal* or an *albergue juvenil* in Argentina. Make sure you're understood. I once spent hours trawling the streets of Tucumán asking for an *albergue*, only to be answered by baffled red faces. A kindly gentleman finally informed me that as far as he was concerned an *albergue* was a place young lovers went for an hour or so. The full name of these love motels is *albergue transitorios*. They are also known as *telos* in the local slang – but you probably won't walk into one by accident as they have obvious names like 'You and Me', red lights and discreet parking.

Estancias: At Home on the Range

To find the real heart of Argentina's Interior, you shouldn't miss out on an opportunity to visit an *estancia*. *Estancia* is the Argentine word for 'ranch', but it can stretch to mean anything from a large country estate of thousands of acres to a small working farm. *Estancias* can be found throughout the Interior, from *yerba mate* plantations in the north to grain and cattle ranches of the pampas and vast sheep stations in Patagonia.

With changing times, many *estancias* are no longer financially self-supporting in the traditional way and, luckily for us, have opened their doors to paying house guests to supplement their income. Here you can observe the life of a working *estancia* – not much changed since their heyday in the mid-19th century – and participate in country pursuits such as riding, polo, canoeing, birdwatching or simply relaxing round the family swimming pool before tucking into a massive *asado*. *Estancias* are ideal weekend breaks for both *porteños* and expats who long to get away from the frenzied buzz of the city.

Houses and Apartments

Of course, if you're planning on staying in Argentina for a certain amount of time, you will doubtless consider renting or even buying an apartment. Like all transactions in Argentina, contacts will be crucial. Without them, renting can become a strategic nightmare. You will be required to procure two guarantors (two separate people who are home-owners and Argentine residents who will be legally bound to pay your rent and bills should you fail to do so), two months' rent in advance, and two months' rent as deposit. Argentines themselves bank on family members to act as their guarantors, so it's seen as a good idea to stay on amicable terms with your parents before you move out. If you've come to Argentina for business, hopefully your company will volunteer to act as your guarantor.

For a cheaper and more straightforward option – generally without the need of a guarantor – look for a room in a shared house. These may be advertised in the classified section of newspapers and also by an easy-to-spot sign saying *Habitación Disponible*, stuck on the wall of the house in question.

It's surprisingly difficult to find apartments in the *Friends* style, where a young group of friends share an apartment, without the beady eye of an oldie looking over them. This is because children and young people tend to live with their families until they are married. To move out prematurely still raises eyebrows and could imply that you have fallen out with your parents. I was lucky enough to find a room in a shared flat with seven other 20-somethings in Buenos Aires' down-trodden San Telmo neighbourhood. (None of them had fallen out with their parents.) It didn't matter that I had no stereo; the nightclub downstairs played great salsa from Wednesday through Saturday and if I switched off my bedroom light I got flashing disco lights to boot. (Fine for me but maybe not so good for others.) Things got even better when upon further exploration I discovered I lived on the same street as a top tango bar, several all-night cafés and the president! With Argentina's rigid grid system, streets can run for several kilometres and tend to keep the same name for their entire length.

The highlight of our building, however, was a fantastic gold and black cage-like elevator, which must have been at least 100 years old, that torpedoed its passengers up and down to the accompaniment of alarming noises. Although maximum capacity stated three people, as many as five of us would frequently pile in, and because of the complicated weight system we would plummet to the ground floor or groan upwards to the fifth. On particularly bad days we would even free-fall for several metres. I stopped using 'The Cage' altogether after reading a horrifying statistic that claimed someone crashes to their death in a broken elevator every two hours in Argentina.

Maybe it's the precarious elevator system that causes old houses and apartments to be religiously avoided by Argentines, who hanker after the new, modern apartments. Old buildings are rather seen as secondhand goods, and, finances permitting, are generally shunned. Understandably, considering the idea of being lumbered with the bill when the crumbling walls, questionable plumbing and roof finally give way. Still, if you keep your eyes open, you could pick up a nice turn-of-the-century house for a fraction of the cost of a small modern apartment in a trendy neighbourhood.

If buying, you may consider moving into a respectable barrio, but make sure you do your homework first. There are ideal-looking houses sited next to *villas miseria* (Argentina's shantytowns) that have been on the market for years. Don't be the clot who eventually buys one of these unless you're planning to stay there for good.

Guide to House Prices and Rentals

The following is a rough guide to house/apartment sale and rental prices in Argentina. Prices will be highest in Buenos Aires, but you can count on the equivalent in the Interior at around 20 per cent less. The guide is based on two-bedroom house/apartments in Buenos Aires. Monthly rent is nearly always one per cent of the house price.

Top Neighbourhoods

Palermo Chico, Recoleta (near the British Embassy and Hyatt Hotel), Avenida Liberatador. A two-bedroom apartment would set you back upwards from US$150,000, while a palatial house in Barrio Parque (millionaires' row) with swimming pool, terraces and car elevator would cost several million. You could probably rent a four- or five-bedroom house (with pool and garage) for about US$5,000 a month.

Middle Neighbourhoods

Belgrano, other parts of Palermo, Nuñez, the northern outskirts of Buenos Aires from Vicente Lopez to San Isidro. A two-bedroom apartment here goes from about US$70,000 upwards.

Bottom Neighbourhoods

San Telmo, Flores, Once, Caballito, Congreso and Boca: many of these neighbourhoods, Boca in particular, are still considered fairly dangerous after dark. A two-bedroom apartment would be in the region of US$50,000 plus. You may find something cheaper.

ELECTRICITY SUPPLY

Electricity is supplied at 220 volts, 50 cycles AC. Plug fittings are either the European-style two round pins or the flat three-pin type. Adapters are available locally. Lamp fittings are the screw type.

RECYCLING

Just because that old filing cabinet or those worn-out curtains no longer appeal to you, it doesn't mean no one else will have them. Argentines are great recyclers (but not necessarily in the sense of paper and plastic), and what's old hat for you could be just what someone else is looking for. At night, many poorer folk and people from the *villas miserias* stroll through city streets looking for discarded items they can put to good use. So before you chuck something away, think again. Put it out on the pavement last thing at night and by morning, I guarantee you, it will probably have found a new home.

A different and much more up-market type of recycling can be found in the country's wonderful antique shops. Don't miss out on a chance to browse through San Telmo's Sunday market.

PET CARE

If the kindness of nationalities is judged by the way they treat their pets, then Argentines would be up there at the top. There seems to be a sort of adopt-a-stray policy in force in Argentina, and many locals have taken upon themselves the task of providing regular supplies of food and water to those cats and dogs that have fallen by the wayside.

Richer pets will be spoilt for choice, with a wealth of topnotch poodle parlours to pick from. And for those of you with dogs who just don't have the time to take them for walkies, there is no shortage of professional dog walkers, known as *pasaperros*, in Buenos Aires. The sight of these dog walkers, tangled in a web of leads with a dozen dogs at the other end of them, provides a wonderfully comical sight and has become a very *porteño* image. Oh, but do watch where you step on the sidewalk!

Photo: Jamie Grant

A husky pup gets a cuddle in Tierra del Fuego.

EDUCATION

At 96.2 per cent Argentina can boast one of Latin America's highest literacy rates, but faith in the public education system remains shaky. If they can afford it, Argentines will send their children to private schools rather than the state institutions. Part of the blame lies with lack of funds. Teachers' pay is lousy, averaging just US$300 dollars a month, and as a result many teachers work at two or three different schools to make ends meet. It's not unheard of for a teacher to simply not turn up for a class; chances are they're at their other job.

Education from preschool to university level is available free of charge in Argentina and is compulsory for all children up to 14 years of age. Primary school enrolment is close to 100 per cent of the school-age population, but dropout rates in secondary schools are relatively high (in 1996, 67 per cent of the school-age population was enrolled in secondary schools). Secondary education lasts from five to seven years. The standard certificate is the *bachillerato*, which takes on average five years to complete. A technical or agricultural *bachillerato* takes six years to complete.

There are some 20 private universities in Argentina, although the country's 31 state universities are considered good on the whole, and for certain careers, such as medicine and architecture, better than private universities. State universities are free; a private university charges about US$350 a month, sometimes more. The standard of education will not necessarily be better in a private university, but facilities, organisation and administration are considered relatively superior – lessons, for example, generally start on time. Another advantage of the private system is that degree courses can be completed in five years while state universities require at least six years.

Most students continue living at home with their parents during college and so tend to go to universities in their home city. The general exception to this rule is the University of Córdoba. Argentina's oldest university takes an estimated six out of ten students from outside the area. Out-of-town students camp down in small *pensións* or boarding houses, sharing a single room with as many as five others.

Many students work to support themselves through university, especially by the time they reach their fourth, fifth or sixth year, even if they are still living at home with their parents.

As you might well imagine, Argentine students have a touch of the revolutionary about them – this is, after all, Che Guevara's homeland. (He studied medicine at Córdoba.) So don't be surprised to see Marxist book fairs, communist banners and cooperative-run cafés in the university grounds. This is not that much different from universities in North America or Europe and it's unlikely that they are about to take up the armed struggle. Still, when the government tried to cut the education budget in 1999, thousands of students staged angry protests throughout the country to demonstrate against the cuts and the government had to quickly backtrack.

Parents who don't want to totally immerse their children in the Argentine education system can choose from several private primary and secondary schools in Argentina. Many of these are bilingual and lessons are taught in English and Spanish (and other European languages). Lessons in state schools are always in Spanish.

To enrol in a state school or university you will need either a residence or student visa, both obtainable from your local Argentine consulate at a charge of about US$120. (Addresses of bilingual schools are listed in the Strategic Directory, Chapter 10.)

MONEY, MONEY, MONEY

As a result of the 1991 convertibility law that pegged the Argentine peso to the US dollar, everything comes at a price and Argentina is, for now, one of the most expensive countries in South America. Cash, therefore, will be a priority. Thankfully, access is fairly straightforward and you won't even need a calculator to work out the exchange rate. Many places accept US dollars in lieu of the Argentine peso, although it is always polite to ask if this is all right first. At one stage there was even talk of ditching the peso altogether and adopting US dollars as the national currency. This went down like a lead balloon with *argentinidad* proponents. Bank accounts – and practically all savings accounts – tend to be denominated in US dollars.

Banks, Bureaux de Changes (*Casas de Cambio*) and Automated Teller Machines (ATMs) deal in US dollars and Argentine pesos. You can get away with handing over torn and dirty pesos, but dollars must to be in perfect condition. Cashing traveller's cheques can be quite difficult and the charges are often high. Many banks refuse to change certain types of traveller's cheques – if any at all. (American Express is widely considered the best.) ATMs throw out a confusing stream of Spanish, but often have an English translation and are unlikely to gobble your card. The green-and-yellow *LINK* sign or the red *Banelco* sign indicates machines that accept most of the major credit cards including Visa, MasterCard, Diners Club International and Cirrus.

You may also consider opening a local bank account. Provided you have all the correct documentation, including a residence visa and a valid passport, this should be easy. As in all things, an unexpected problem could arise. For example, one foreign visitor's efforts to open an account were rejected because his passport number was 'too long'. His advice: 'Persist. It is possible.' Recommended banks include Bank Boston, HSBC Roberts, Banco Francés, Banco Galicia, Citibank and Banco Rio. Note that you may be charged a monthly fee for the privilege of having a current account or even a savings account.

Now for the biggest money frustration: no one ever seems to have any change. At times a 50 or a 100 peso note is as good as worthless. If a shopkeeper refuses to accept your note and demands that you come up with smaller change, stand your ground! They'll probably produce the change in the end. At smaller kiosks you may be encouraged to accept your change in the form of sweets or candy if the shopkeeper is out of small coins. Peso notes come in denominations of 100, 50, 20, 10, 5 and 2 pesos. There are coins for one peso and also for 50, 25, 10 and 5 centavos. No one ever has any 5 centavo coins so things are usually rounded off to the nearest 10 centavos.

Forgeries of both peso and dollar banknotes are common in Argentina, so take care when dealing with large amounts of cash.

The provinces of Jujuy, Salta and Tucumán use both pesos and a system known as *bonos*. *Bonos* look to all intents and purposes like useless scraps of paper and outside the province of issue they are no more than that (so make sure you leave the province without them). Within the province of issue, however, they are valid as currency.

Tipping and Bargaining

If a service charge is included on your restaurant bill, you are still expected to tip 5 per cent. If no service charge is included, add a tip of 10 per cent. In *parrillas* there is often a box where you can tip the *asador*. It is sweaty, hard work and, as you will undoubtedly be served such exquisite beef, any tip is well-deserved.

Taxi drivers do not expect to get tips. In fact, the fare may well be rounded down rather than up. But if your *tachero* has been especially helpful, a tip will be appreciated.

Ushers in cinemas and theatres expect a tip (about 10 per cent of the ticket price). And they should certainly be tipped should you take a programme or arrive late and have to be led to your seat in the dark.

Other people to tip include hairdressers; the man who loads your baggage into the hold in buses; porters in airports, bus stations, train stations and hotels; gas station attendants (if they fill the tank, clean the windshield or check the oil); and delivery servicemen.

Bargaining is not common in Argentina but you can ask for – and expect – a 10 per cent discount if paying cash in many shops. Very occasionally taxi drivers are open to pre-negotiated prices.

Paying Bills

If possible, pay all your bills as soon as they arrive. Should you miss the payment deadline, you will enter a world of bureaucratic chaos. All bills must be paid in person at one of the places stated on the back of the bill. Put simply, the later you leave it to pay, the shorter your list of places where you can pay becomes. Ultimately, you will have to go directly to the gas board, electricity board or wherever and queue with hoards of others who had also left it to the last minute. There is a relatively new service, appropriately called *Pago Facil* (Easy Pay); you can now also pay your bills at places where this sign is shown instead of at a bank where queues can get ridiculously long.

MAIL

Outgoing airmail letters take about five days to reach the United States, seven days to reach Europe, and anything up to weeks in the other direction. Letters can be sent from post offices, larger hotels and mailboxes on the street – these are painted dark blue in the Interior and red in Buenos Aires. Incoming mail can be received at your home or office address; alternatively you can open a PO box at the *correo central* (post office) for three, six or 12 months at a time. The post office is open Monday to Friday from 8:00 am to 8:00 pm and on Saturday between 8:00 am and 1:00 pm.

Hopefully you'll be home when the postman arrives with a parcel. Otherwise, you must queue in the *correo central* where you will be given an eight-digit number. Even native Spanish speakers have trouble making out the numbers that are announced muffled through a loudspeaker. When your number's called, pick up your parcel from a counter where it might be opened in front of you by a suspicious bureaucrat. 'The whole experience was so humiliating,' said an English friend, 'that I asked my family to stop sending me things.'

It is not completely unknown for post, in both directions, to go astray. If this worries you, send your mail from a post office; to be doubly safe, send it registered. Major international courier companies, including DHL, Federal Express and UPS, are represented in Argentina.

TELEPHONES

The cause of much fury and frustration, Argentina's telephone system is getting over its teething period and is finally on the road to recovery. Dialling a number is still often a matter of luck; you may reach your destination first time, but more frequently get a stranger growling that you're *equivocado* (wrong). Doubtless as a result partly of years of crossed lines and largely the expense of having a fixed line installed, Argentines have lapped up the mobile phone market. Argentina now has one of the highest number of mobile phones per capita in the world. The possession of the cell phone, rather like car ownership, is something of a status symbol. Argentines tend to wear them slung in holsters on their belts like urban cowboys, proud and ready to whip them out at the slightest high-pitched shrill.

It doesn't matter if you don't have your own mobile or even your own telephone line, as the country is well served by telephone centres (*locutorios*). There is at least one *locutorio* in each small town and hundreds in each city. The rates are far more competitive than calling from hotels – which add significant surcharges to calls and faxes – and the procedure couldn't be simpler: enter a numbered booth, make your call and settle up at the manned desk on your way out. Most of the larger *locutorios* have also installed Internet and e-mail facilities.

All local telephone numbers since January 1999 have to be prefixed with the number 4, and all area codes with a 1, 2 or 3 (after the 0) depending on the region. Buenos Aires city has an extra 1 in the area code (it is now 011 rather than 01). The southern provinces of San Juan, Mendoza, San Luis, La Pampa, Buenos Aires, Neuquén, Río Negro, Chubut, Santa Cruz and Tierra del Fuego now have a 2 in the area code. (For example, the code for Río Gallegos, previously 0966, is now 02966.) The northern provinces of Jujuy, Salta, Tucumán, Catamarca, La Rioja, Santiago del Estero, Córdoba, Formosa, Chaco, Santa Fe, Entre Ríos, Corrientes and Misiones now include a 3 in their area code. (For example, Córdoba's code is now 0351 rather than 051.) Many information sources and directories have not been updated, so make sure you add the extra digit when dialling.

A heavy rainstorm can still wipe out telephone lines, along with the electricity supply, for hours, even in Buenos Aires.

SHOPPING

Perhaps one of the reasons Argentines devote so much time to shopping is that it can be so much fun. Purchases, however insignificant, will be painstakingly wrapped in coloured tissue paper and ribbons and popped into bags along with the shop's calling card. Nearly all purchases can be delivered free of charge to your house and if you can't immediately foot the bill, a string of attractive options allows you to pay it off in interest-free instalments over many months.

They can look an intimidating bunch through the window, but shop assistants in Argentina couldn't be friendlier and more helpful. Window-shopping is tricky though, as you will be pounced upon as soon as you walk through the door and encouraged to purchase.

Clothes shopping for women can be traumatic. Those who take a 'medium' in the United States or Europe will find they are 'large' or even 'extra large' in Argentina. I have read one horror story of a girl who was entering a shop and was told to not even bother coming in as they had nothing in her size. Clothes are geared towards the Twiggy look where hipbones and ribcages are all the rage. Impossibly thin shop-window dummies have clothes pinned onto them to stop them falling off. This is especially the case in the flashy shopping malls where, if you're above size ten, you can suffer a harrowing experience. Just as you're fleeing, near to tears because nothing fits, you'll be cornered by a stick insect thrusting a pamphlet from a 'slim centre' into your hand offering interest-free liposuction. But don't let shopping malls put you off. Larger-sized clothing is available away from chain stores and shopkeepers often add that personal touch.

As they do in other product and service areas. Pharmacists, for example, will listen patiently to your symptoms, diagnose and pre scribe, even (surprisingly) antibiotics. This may be a remarkably effective way of cutting out the middleman, but if it's serious medicine you're after, ideally you should go and see a doctor first.

Another personal favourite has to be the owners of ice cream parlours, who cleverly encourage you to taste spoonfuls of irresistible new flavours for free. There also seems to be a certain skill involved in balancing enormous amounts of ice cream into tiny cones. The result is a top heavy but deliciously generous serving; many visitors to Argentina claim the ice cream is the best they've ever eaten.

Shops open between 9 and 10 in the morning and close around 6, 7 or even 8 in the evening. Shopping malls stay open even later. In the provinces, shops may well close between 1:00 pm and 4:00 pm for the siesta. Those that do will probably stay open late into the evening. Supermarkets may well remain open as late as 10:30 pm. In tune with the country's party atmosphere there's a chain of supermarkets called Disco. These are buzzing late at night when everyone seems to be out frantically last-minute shopping for the typically late-night meal.

Incidentally, Argentina uses the metric system. Shoe and clothing sizes tend to be European although Argentines are increasingly using the English terms *extra large*, *large*, *medium*, *small* and of course *extra small*.

Kioskos

What would Argentina be without *el kiosko*? These wonderful local street stalls are the heart and soul of Argentina's cities, stocking just about anything you can think of – from hot dogs and cigarettes to chocolate and *yerba mate* – and often staying open long after the other shops have shut. After some time, your local kiosk vendor will become your best friend and if you don't have the right change, he'll probably just tell you to come back tomorrow. *Kioskos* vary in shape and size. They may be simple holes in the wall or quite elaborate affairs with plastic chairs and tables inside. The green tin newspaper kiosks are everybody's favourite, selling practically every newspaper, magazine, map and leaflet you can think of. And if they don't stock what you are looking for, then in true *kiosko* style, they will order it for you tomorrow.

Books and Media

Thanks to Argentina's considerable Anglophile community, English reading material is readily available, although it may come at a price. If you poke around into the further recesses of Argentina's famous bookshops you'll also come across books in French, Portuguese, German and Italian. There is an English-language daily newspaper, the *Buenos Aires Herald*, with good coverage of national and international news, finance and sports; on Sundays it has the *Guardian* weekly supplement. You'll also be able to pick up English and American magazines from *Vogue* to the *Economist* at newspaper kiosks in the larger cities. If you read Spanish, an even larger literary world awaits you. Newspaper kiosks are packed with every possible type of magazine from *Tango* to *Travel*. Businessmen will want to

Photo: Jamie Grant

A glimpse into one of Argentina's late-night bookshops.

devour the pages of the business dailies *Ambito Financiero* or *El Cronista*. Buenos Aires' bookshops, many of which stock second-hand books, are justifiably famous and open late into the night. You will be perfectly welcome to hang out for hours among the shelves and might even get away with reading an entire book without having to buy it. Buenos Aires also hosts South America's largest book fair in April, the *Fería Internacional del Libro*.

Cable television is popular in Argentina, but national TV stations are also good with amusing chat shows, riveting *telenovelas* (soap operas), current affairs documentaries and news. If a football match is being televised, however, think twice before trying to change channels – especially if there's a man in the room.

Argentina is also well ensconced on-line. Most businesses have e-mail and Internet access, as do many individuals. There are dozens of Internet service providers (ISPs) to choose from. Local Argentine ISPs are listed in the Strategic Directory, Chapter 10.

WHAT TO WEAR

If you plan to cavort with Argentina's rich and famous, you're going to need a wardrobe to rival James Bond's. Argentines – *porteños* in particular – are extremely fashion-conscious so come prepared to be eyed up and down. Men will find a suit and tie useful for formal occasions. Some nightclubs, casinos, restaurants and theatres have a dress code. A dinner jacket or an evening dress is also standard wear for a gala night at the opera or theatre. Should you take to the ski slopes, besides warm clothing you'll need something great to wear in the evening. Women who intend to dance the tango will find fishnet stockings and high heels indispensable.

Should you plan to see more than one season in Argentina your wardrobe will expand further. The fierce *sudestada* or southeasterly wind that blows up the Río de la Plata carries a considerable nip in the air as far north as Buenos Aires. In summer (November to March) temperatures can easily reach the high 30s (°C), and with Buenos

Aires' high humidity it can be sweltering. So play it safe and come prepared for all meteorological eventualities. If you plan to go down to Patagonia or Tierra del Fuego, even in mid-summer (January and February) you'll need a large down jacket, woollen gloves, hat and, most importantly, something to keep the interminable wind out.

Don't forget to pack bikinis and shorts for beach outings. Beach wear is considerably more conservative than in Brazil. Girls, don't even *think* about going topless. The one time a group of avant-garde beach babes tried to do this it created the most uproarious scandal and the TV cameras had a field day. Nightclubbing, however, can be as raunchy as you like. If in doubt, overdress rather than underdress and go for glamour every time. You are not going to get splashed in red paint if you wear a fur coat in Buenos Aires.

TIMEKEEPING

Argentines are not big on punctuality, so try not to get too stressed if you are kept waiting. There's always *mañana*. In fact, arriving at the appointed hour could be a social gaffe. For example, if you are invited to someone's home for dinner at 9:00 pm, don't even think of arriving before 9:30 pm, unless of course you want to catch your hostess in the bath. Likewise, it's generally a good idea to be fashionably late for parties, drinks, nightclubs and other social events. There are exceptions: you'll probably want to arrive on time for organised events such as a concert, even though these are not guaranteed to kick off on time. In a business setting, punctuality on your part is important even if your host rolls in late.

Every so often you get the distinct feeling that actually it's the 'done thing' to be seen as the last to arrive at a social gathering or even to board an aeroplane. Maybe, you think, they are really twirling their thumbs at home waiting for 3:00 am to roll on. But perhaps the most likely reason for this tardiness is that Argentines spend literally hours grooming and getting ready to go out. The end product is, without exception, always fabulous.

A punctilious English friend of mine, married to an Argentine, gets around this timekeeping problem by telling his wife that he wants to leave the house at least an hour before he actually intends to. That way his wife has plenty of time to get ready (and is what she believes to be fashionably late) and he gets to leave on time.

La Siesta

One of the greatest joys of life in Latin America is the siesta. This is a period that lasts several hours in the early afternoon, when everything is put on standby – shops close, businesses shut down and everybody goes home for a snooze or just to relax. The hotter the region, the more entrenched the siesta. And although the siesta has become a rarity in Buenos Aires and other big cities in Argentina, it is still a thoroughly important institution in the Interior.

HEALTH AND SAFETY

For years, Argentina could proudly boast of being one of the safest Latin American nations, provided you didn't get inside a car. During 1997, 49 people were killed on public roads in Madrid, 62 in Paris and 73 in Rome. In the city of Buenos Aires 423 people were killed. I don't mean to scare you with gruesome statistics, but do be careful and keep your wits about you at all times – this applies to both pedestrians and drivers.

It is estimated that half of Argentina's annual road deaths could have been avoided had people been wearing their seatbelt at the time. Seatbelts are required by law, but generally people wear one only when they're within sight of a policeman. If you do decide to do the sensible thing and buckle up you will probably have to dig the seatbelts out from down the back of the car seats (if they're there at all) and brace yourself for sidelong glances that imply you're being cowardly and un-macho.

Unfortunately Argentina's roads are no longer the only danger for locals and visitors. Armed hold-ups and shoot-outs, although not a common occurrence, are not unheard of now, even in the smarter neighbourhoods. Gangs of armed thieves have been known to walk into restaurants and demand everyone's valuables. The worsening economic crisis and ever-widening gap between rich and poor have been singled out to blame. Always seek local advice on what and where is safe and what is considered unsafe.

Also be on your guard against bag snatchers and pickpockets, especially in crowded or touristy areas and in the big cities. The classic robbery is the 'mustard trick' – someone will squirt a bottle of sauce (usually mustard) over your clothes and an accomplice then offers to hold your bag while you clean yourself up. They then walk off with your bag and you are left with egg on your face, so to speak.

Don't even think about taking a handbag along to a football match. Football games can be dangerous and many fans are armed with knives and even guns. Argentina must be one of the few countries in the world where you face getting lynched for being in the wrong place at the wrong time while supporting the wrong team. (See Chapter 7 for more details.)

Health Hazards

The humidity in Buenos Aires (averaging 76 per cent) will make the winters seem colder and the summers hotter. Then there is the pollution to contend with. The newspaper *La Clarin* runs a daily chart of carbon monoxide pollution levels in Buenos Aires, which always seem to hover precariously close and frequently over the maximum tolerable line. It makes for interesting reading even though you can't do much about it. Asthma sufferers and those with sinus or bronchial problems may have trouble with heat and pollution in Buenos Aires and should also be aware that during the dry season unpaved roads can get very dusty indeed.

Always seek local advice before eating seafood, especially shellfish. The red tide (*marea roja*) periodically affects the coast of Argentina. It is deadly and should not be taken lightly.

Creepy Crawlies and other Nasties

Argentines are sticklers for fumigation and men in white coats make regular house visits to spray into those dark corners. In Buenos Aires, they're usually after ants and cockroaches, which are quite a problem in the summer. South America's really nasty creepy crawlies don't make it as far south as Buenos Aires or Patagonia.

Further north, however, where it's hotter, and especially in low-lying tropical areas, it's advisable to take malaria pills. Obviously the best approach is to avoid being bitten by mosquitoes altogether. Dengue fever, which is prevalent in some areas, is also transmitted by mosquitoes. Other dangers in the north include leishmaniasis and Chagas' disease. Chagas' disease is transmitted through the bite of the vinchuca beetle, causing arteries to harden and long-term complications that eventually lead to death. The beetle likes *adobe* buildings with dirt floors and decrepit roofs and usually comes out at night, so avoid sleeping in such dwellings if you can. If you have no choice, tuck up your feet (the beetles go for these) and use a mosquito net. If you think you've been bitten by a vinchuca, seek medical advice immediately. If you've been in a malarial area and show symptoms even as late as a year after your trip, see a doctor immediately.

AIDS

Acquired Immune Deficiency Syndrome (AIDS) was first reported in Argentina in 1982 and the number of known cases has grown from 720 in 1991 to 1,624 in 1995. Underreporting is considered to be very high – the incidence of AIDS is estimated to be 40 per cent higher than reported levels. The majority of Aids victims are in the 20–34 age group and an increasingly higher number of women are being infected; 21.9 per cent of cases in 1996 were women. Leading causes of infection are through intravenous drug use, sexual transmission and an HIV-positive mother. However, the HIV virus can also be contracted through medical and dental procedures involving the use of infected hypodermic or blood transfusion equipment. Where possible seek medical treatment only after consulting your embassy. Condoms, which can prevent the transmission of HIV and other sexually transmitted diseases, are widely available in Argentina despite this being a Catholic country.

Vaccinations

You are not legally required to have any vaccinations before entering Argentina, but the following vaccines are usually recommended for those travelling to the region.

- Hepatitis A or immune globulin (IG).
- Rabies, if you expect to be exposed to wild or domestic animals through work or recreation.
- Typhoid, particularly if you plan on spending time in underdeveloped areas or are an adventurous eater.
- Yellow fever, recommended if travelling outside urban areas although it's considered a very low risk. It's a good idea to bring your yellow fever certificate with you should you plan to travel to or arrive from infected neighbouring countries as you might be required to show proof that you have been vaccinated.
- Tetanus booster.

See your doctor at least 4–6 weeks before your trip to allow time for immunisation to take effect.

Doctors and Medical Emergencies

In larger cities, you probably won't have too much trouble finding a doctor who speaks English (addresses of hospitals with English-speaking staff are listed in the Strategic Directory, Chapter 10). Many Argentines and most expats, if possible, sign up with a private health programme which covers medical and dental costs and includes an ambulance service. There are both private and state hospitals (private hospitals undoubtedly provide the better service). There is also a national ambulance emergency service (tel: 107), but the running joke is that it's so slow you'll probably die of old age before it arrives.

GETTING THERE AND AWAY

A valid passport is required for all those wishing to enter Argentina.

Entry visas are not required for tourists from Andorra, Australia, Austria, Barbados, Belgium, Bolivia, Brazil, Canada, Chile, Colombia, Costa Rica, Croatia, Denmark, Dominican Republic, Ecuador, El Salvador, Finland, France, Germany, Great Britain, Greece, Guatemala, Haiti, Honduras, Hong Kong, Hungary, Ireland, Israel, Italy, Jamaica, Japan, Liechtenstein, Luxembourg, Malaysia, Malta, Mexico, Monaco, the Netherlands, Nicaragua, Norway, New Zealand, Panama, Paraguay, Peru, Poland, Portugal, Slovenia, Spain, South Africa, Sweden, Switzerland, Turkey, Uruguay, the United States, Venezuela and Yugoslavia. But visitors from these countries must obtain a free tourist card valid for 90 days upon entering Argentina. Tourist cards may be unavailable at smaller border crossings. Don't worry if you never get a tourist card, or even lose your tourist card. In a country where bureaucracy is alive and kicking, immigration guards can still be surprisingly relaxed and you can fill one out on departure.

A visa is required prior to departure for citizens of all the countries not mentioned above, and is available from the local Argentine consulate. The official line is that all visitors on business require a visa, but most business travellers who plan to spend no more than 90 days in the country enter on the tourist card, thus avoiding unnecessary red tape. If you think you're going to attract a lot of attention because of the nature of your business or plan to stay for more than 90 days, you should obtain a valid business visa before you leave.

Long-term work and residence permits are also available but you should try to contact your local Argentine consulate well in advance of your departure. This visa will enable you to get hold of an Argentine ID card, which you'll need to open bank accounts and pay taxes.

Visitors to Argentina are allowed to bring in up to 2 litres of spirits, 100 cigarettes and 30 cigars tax-free. No duty is levied on clothing, personal effects or used electronic items, but you may encounter problems if you are bringing in duplicate articles.

Finally, if you were born in Argentina but hold current citizenship in another country don't leap onto that Aerolineas Argentinas flight without first clearing your status. Under Argentine law all those born in Argentina except children of visiting diplomats are Argentine citizens for life and thus subject to the military draft and other obligations. Obligatory military service, however, was abolished in 1994.

— Chapter Ten —

STRATEGIC DIRECTORY

Contacts are everything in Argentina. You can never know enough people and their phone numbers. In this country strings are pulled, friends of friends and cousins of cousins called up to help you out. If you arrive cold and contactless, the following list of names, addresses and practical information should give you a jump-start.

PHONES, FAXES AND ADDRESSES
Since January 1999, all telephone numbers and area codes in Argentina include new digits (see 'Telephones' in Chapter 9). Directories and information sources may not be up-to-date, so you should double-

check any old information. All the numbers listed in this chapter contain these new digits. Argentina's international country code is ++54. National codes are given in parenthesis; (011) is Buenos Aires.

In addresses, the number follows the street name, a four-digit postal code precedes the city name, and the province name comes last. *Capital Federal* or *CF* is Buenos Aires city, to distinguish it from Buenos Aires province.

Common Address Terms and Abbreviations

Avenida, Av or Avda	Avenue
Bs.As or BA	Buenos Aires
Calle	Street
Capital Federal or CF	Buenos Aires (city)
Casilla (de Correo) or CC	Post Office Box
Codigal Postal or CP	Post Code
Edificio or Edif	Building
Esquina or Esq	Corner
Oficina or Of	Office
Piso or P	Floor
Planta Baja or PB	Ground floor
Provincia	Province
Sin Numero or s/n	No number
Telf	Telephone

EMERGENCY NUMBERS
Police: 101
Fire: 100
Ambulance: 107
Environmental Emergency: 105
Coast Guard: 106

All these can be called from across the country free of charge and there is no need to dial an area code first. For telephone directory inquiries call 110, or consult the local Yellow Pages.

BUSINESS CONTACTS

Organisations and departments of interest to business visitors:

Cámara Argentina de Comercio (Argentine Chamber of Commerce)
Av. L.N. Alem 36
(1003) Capital Federal
Tel: (011) 4331 8055
Fax: (011) 4331 8051

Bolsa de Comercio de Buenos Aires (Buenos Aires Stock Exchange)
Saramiento 299, Piso 1
(1353) Capital Federal
Tel: (011) 4316 7000

Asociación de Importadores y Exportadores (Association of Importers and Exporters)
Av. Belgrano 124, Piso 1
(1092) Capital Federal
Tel: (011) 4342 0010

Ministerio de Relaciones Exteriores, Comercio Internacional y Culto (Ministry of Foreign Affairs, International Trade and Worship)
Reconquista 1088
(1003) Capital Federal
Tel/Fax: (011) 4311 0071

Union Industrial Argentina
L.N. Alem 1067
(1001) Capital Federal
Tel: (011) 4313 2012

Fundación Exportar (Trade Information and Opportunities)
Reconquista 1098
(1003) Capital Federal
Tel: (011) 4315 4125

Fundación Invertir
Bartolomé Mitre 326
Edif. Banco Nación, Piso 1, Of. 109
(1036) Capital Federal
Tel/Fax: (011) 4342 7723
(A private organisation formed by CEOs of leading Argentine enterprises and top government officials, established to promote investments in Argentina of local and foreign firms. It operates in close coordination with the Undersecretariat for Investment.)

Dirección General Impositiva (Argentine Tax Bureau)
Avenida Paseo Colón 635
Capital Federal
Tel: (011) 4331 7807

HOSPITALS

The following private hospitals have English-speaking staff. In each neighbourhood, pharmacies take turns to remain open at night, so you can get hold of medicines and prescriptions round the clock. They are advertised daily in local newspapers under *Farmacias del Turno.*

Hospital Britanico (British Hospital)
Perdriel 74
(1280) Capital Federal
Tel: (011) 4309 6400
(English spoken)

Hospital Aleman (German Hospital)
Pueyreddon 1640
(1118) Capital Federal
Tel: (011) 4821 1700
(English and German spoken)

Hospital Italiano (Italian Hospital)
Gascón 450
Capital Federal
Tel: (011) 4981 5010
(English and Italian spoken)

Hospital Central
Alem y Salta s/n
(5500) Mendoza
Tel: (0261) 4490500
(English spoken)

SCHOOLS

Lessons in these private schools are conducted in Spanish and English and may follow the British or American curriculum:

Asociación Escuela Lincoln
(mixed, kindergarten, primary, secondary)
Andres Frreyra 4073
(1636) La Lucilia
Buenos Aires
Tel: (011) 4794 9400

Belgrano Day School (mixed, secondary)
Juramento 3035
(1428) Belgrano
Buenos Aires
Tel: (011) 47810011

Buenos Aires English High School (mixed, kindergarten, primary)
Av. Melian 1880
(1430) Belgrano
Buenos Aires
Tel: (011) 4552 6778

Northlands School (girls only, kindergarten, primary, secondary)
Roma 1248
(1636) Olivos
Buenos Aires
Tel: (011) 4711 0011

Saint Andrew's Scots School
(mixed, kindergarten, primary, secondary, university)
Roque Saenz Pena 601
(1636) Olivos
Buenos Aires
Tel: (011) 4790 8032

San Andres (mixed, kindergarten, primary, secondary)
Joaquin V. Gonzalez 630
(5500) Mendoza
Tel: (0261) 4250824

St George's College
(mixed, kindergarten, primary, secondary, boarding option)
Guido 800
(1878) Quilmes
Buenos Aires
Tel: (011) 42573472

St George's College North
(mixed, kindergarten, primary, secondary)
Comodoro Rivadavia y
Don Bosco s/n
(1613) Los Polvorines
Buenos Aires
Tel: (011) 4663 2495

Spanish Study Programmes

Academias Pitman
Av. Santa Fe 2517
Capital Federal
Tel: (011) 4821 3763

Berlitz Centro de Idiomas
Av. Cabildo 2261
Capital Federal
Tel: (011) 4788 9998

Brooklyn Bridge S.A.
Sarmiento 517
Capital Federal
Tel: (011) 4394 2366

Code Servicio Linguistico
Junin 1255
Capital Federal
Tel: (011) 4823 2609

EF Educación Internacional
Arenales 319
Capital Federal
Tel: (011) 4815 6715

El Lab Taller de Idiomas
Ayacucho 921
Capital Federal
Tel: (011) 4815 5349

Instituto Flott
Av. Alsina 527
Capital Federal
Tel: (011) 4331 0166

Interaction Language Studio
Av. Leandro N. Alem 424
Capital Federal
Tel: (011) 4311 7220

Internexus
Aguero 2391
Capital Federal
Tel: (011) 4804 0220

The University of Buenos Aires holds morning, afternoon and evening Spanish courses for foreigners. For information, registration and placement tests apply to:
Centro Universitario de Idiomas
Av. Cordoba 2636
Capital Federal
Tel: (011) 4816 0964

A number of private instructors advertise daily in the classified section of the *Buenos Aires Herald*.

INTERNET AND E-MAIL SERVICE PROVIDERS

Computers and software are widely available in Argentina and there is no shortage of Internet service providers. The following service providers give national e-mail and Internet access and can be contacted by telephone or through their web pages (in parentheses). For a full up-to-date list, check out the Internet at Thelist.internet.com/countrycode/54/

Abaco Net, Tel: (011) 4921 4331 (www.abaconet.com.ar)
ACT, Tel: (011) 4804 7700 (www.act.net.ar)
Argentina On Line, Tel: (011) 4804 7700 (www.ba.net.ar)
ArSur SA, Tel: (011) 4315 3539 (www.arsur.com)
Ciudad Internet, Tel: (011) 4370 0000 (www.ciudad.com.ar)
House Internet, Tel: (011) 4381 2400 (www.ciudad.com.ar)

Imagine SRL, Tel: (03882) 429111 (www.imagine.com.ar)
Inea Internet, Tel: (011) 4342 7544 (www.inea.com.ar)
Intermedia, Tel: (011) 4312 9444 (www.intermedia.com.ar)
Internet Providers SA, Tel: (011) 4314 6444 (www.interprov.com)
InterRedes SRL, Tel: (0264) 427590 (www.interredes.com.ar)
Interserver, Tel: (011) 4345 0600 (www.interserver.com.ar)
ISP Canopus SA, Tel: (011) 4554 0489 (www.canopus.com.ar)
Los Pinos II, Tel: (011) 4307 0201 (www.pinos.com)
Microstar, Tel: (0800) 555 64276 (www.microstar.com.ar)
Netverk SA, Tel: (0221) 4241049 (www.netverk.com.ar)
Nornet, Tel: (011) 4821 0030 (www.nornet.com.ar)
OneNet SRL, Tel: (0351) 4259200 (www.onenet.com.ar)
Openware, Tel: (011) 4314 0708/(0341) 4249911
    (www.openware.com.ar)
Pccp, Tel: (011) 4962 1469 (www.pccp.com.ar)
Salnet SA, Tel: (0387) 4310475 (www.salnet.com.ar)
Seek Sistemas, Tel: (011) 4374 6118/0027 (www.seek.com.ar)
ServiceNet SRL, Tel: (011) 4304 3200 (www.servicenet.com.ar)
Sion SA, Tel: (011) 4313 2500 (www.sion.com)
SSDNET, Tel: (011) 4343 1500 (www.ssdnet.com.ar)
Statics SA, Tel: (0223) 4920154 (www.statics.com.ar)
Total Internet, Tel: (011) 4826 5732 (www.totalnet.com.ar)
Tournet, Tel: (011) 43264878 (www.tournet.com.ar)
Via Net Works Argentina SA, Tel: (011) 4327 4400
    (www.vianetworks.net.ar)
Virtulizar, Tel: (011) 4431 5334 (www.virtulizar.com)

MAPS

For travel around the country the *Automovil Club Argentino* has good
road maps – tel: (011) 4802 6061. Most newspaper kiosks also sell
good maps of Argentina, its cities and provinces. Look out for brands
such as AUTOMAPA, with concise routes and city maps – Arenales
3651, (1425) Capital Federal, tel/fax: (011) 4833 3033. The *Instituto*

Geográfico Militar (Geographical Military Institute) in Buenos Aires sells satellite images and topographical maps on scales of 1:500,000, 1:250,000 and 1:100,000 – Av. Cabildo 381, Capital Federal, tel: (011) 4576 5576/79, fax: (011) 4576 5509.

If you'll be spending any time in Buenos Aires get the *Lumi* guide – tel: (011) 4522 6017. This indispensable guide gives all the bus routes in Buenos Aires and concise maps of the city. There is also a good section of useful telephone numbers in the back.

TRAVEL AND TOURISM

The *Automovil Club Argentino* (ACA) provides mechanical assistance, insurance, maps, lists of hotels and hostels, tour promotions, a driving school and other advantages for its members. For further information contact:

Automovil Club Argentino
Av. Libertador 1850
(1425) CF
Tel: (011) 4802 6061
Free tel: (0800) 888 9888

Government Tourist Offices

Run by wonderfully helpful, friendly staff who are quite clued up and just waiting for your visit. Tourist offices supply information on every region as well as lists of *casa de familias* (bed and breakfast places) and local *estancias* open to visitors. The central hub for tourism is the *Secretaria de Turismo de la Nación* in Buenos Aires. There are also tourist offices at Ezeiza airport and provincial tourist offices throughout the country. Each province also has an office in Buenos Aires. For further information contact:

Secretaria de Turismo de la Nación
Santa Fe 883
(1059) CF
Tel: (011) 4312 2232/5550

POLO

The Argentine Polo Association
Hipolito Yrigoyen 636, Piso 1, A
(1086) Capital Federal
Tel/Fax: (011) 4343 0972

The website **www.polonet.com.ar** is regularly updated with interviews, tournament news and information on polo clubs and players in Argentina.

TANGO

Academia Nacional del Tango
(National Tango Academy)
Palacio Carlos Gardel
Avda. de Mayo 833
(1084) Capital Federal
Tel: (011) 4345 6968

Visitors are welcome to drop in at this central hub of Argentine tango and pick up leaflets on Buenos Aires' happening tango scene. Tango classes and *milongas* are advertised in *Tanguato* magazine, copies of which are available at the Academy.

CULTURAL QUIZ

And now for a chance to put your newly acquired skills to the test ...

SITUATION ONE

You are invited to drink *yerba mate* with some Argentine friends but
you've still got to get used to the withered bitter taste that reminds
you of boiled straw. Everyone else is partaking like good gauchos.
Do you:

A   Join in?

B   Decline with a polite *gracias*?

C   Tell them 'No way!' and ask incredulously how on earth an entire
nation can be hooked on something so vile?

Comments

An offer of *mate* is a gesture of friendship and a sign of acceptance and therefore should never be rejected, so *A* is always the best response. If you persevere you might actually start enjoying it. If you really can't stomach the brew, then answer *B*. Your Argentine friends will understand you're just being a gringo with bad taste. Never answer *C*. Argentines adore their *mate*. This is not just any old drink, it's a lifestyle and an essential part of Argentina's culture. Don't knock it.

SITUATION TWO

It's August and you've been invited for a few days' skiing in Bariloche, that Aspen of the Andes. The weather forecast predicted lots of snow and freezing temperatures. You plan to fly there and want to take only one small suitcase as hand luggage. What do you pack?

A Woolly jumpers, a down jacket, long johns, gloves and anything else chunky and unattractive. Nothing really matches, but what does it matter, this is the middle of Patagonia and you're going to the mountains! Surely the fashion police won't be there?

B Skimp on warm clothes to leave plenty of space for slinky dresses/dinner jackets, your best party shoes and some alka seltzer.

C One great ski suit and a fantastic evening outfit that will knock the socks off your hosts.

Comments

A, of course, seems to be the obvious choice: August is the height of winter in Argentina and in this neck of the woods things can get quite chilly. But wait a minute! Are you not forgetting that you're in Argentina and must be fairly fashionable at all times – especially in a resort like Bariloche where you're bound to rub shoulders with the *farándula*? Going out is big business in Bariloche; people aren't here just for the skiing but for the string of discos and nights of revelling. You will definitely need something great to wear in the evenings. *B* means you close off your skiing options. *C*'s the ideal solution (although maybe you should pack that alka seltzer after all).

SITUATION THREE

You are attending a carnival party in an old barn off the beaten track somewhere in the northwest. You've just washed your hair and are wearing your best outfit when a member of the opposite sex, whom you've never met before, pinches your bottom and sprays fake snow in your hair. Do you:

A   Dash off and buy a can of spray snow, seek out the perpetrator and gleefully avenge yourself?

B   Book yourself into some psychoanalysis, fearing that you'll never understand male/female relationships?

C   Leave the room in tears?

Comments

Take it as a compliment, but not as a literal come-on. Carnival is a flirtatious time, and Argentines are outrageous flirts. *C* won't get you anywhere, you'll just miss out on a great party where behaviour like this is perfectly acceptable – it only happens once a year after all. Seeing a psychoanalyst, *B*, wouldn't be that inappropriate. You'll be surprised how many other Argentines do – though probably not for these reasons. *A*, of course is the best answer. It's amazing how therapeutic a can of fake snow and a few drinks can be.

SITUATION FOUR

In Argentina on business, you're running on a tight schedule and the current meeting is beginning to drag. Five minutes into the talks you were pretty sure this wasn't for you, you don't want to cut a deal and you have another business appointment lined up across town in 10 minutes. You're starting to feel frustrated and want to leave. Do you:

A   Make a bolt for the door at the first possible moment, murmuring your apologies on your way out?

B   Let the chief Argentine in the group bring the meeting to an end, remain for a few more minutes of small talk, and roll up 15 minutes late for your next appointment?

C Keep glancing at your watch and eventually – when they haven't got the message – stalk out in a huff?

Comments

A is not a good choice. By running off, you're implying that your next engagement is more important than the present company and it will be taken as an insult. *C* would be a big mistake. You're burning your bridges if you leave under a black cloud. The Argentine business world is a fairly close-knit community and word of your attitude is likely to get around, closing doors to you in future business negotiations. *B* may be the only possible solution. In the future you'll know not to schedule back-to-back meetings.

SITUATION FIVE

A friend invites you to the local *milonga* in San Telmo. The catch is, you've never danced the tango before. You are scared of making an idiot of yourself, so do you:

A Throw your inhibitions aside, rush out and get dressed in the full tango kit (fishnets/trilby, scarlet lipstick/wet look hair gel), then leap onto the dance floor as soon as you arrive?

B Accept, secretly knowing that absolutely no one is going to get you on that dance floor?

C Politely decline the offer and spend the evening kicking your heels at home, miserable?

Comments

None of the answers is a real winner. Only absolute wallflowers should choose option *C*. Tango isn't the exclusive preserve of professional ballroom dancers. Besides, a *milonga* is a great place to drink, people-watch *and* dance. *A* may be overly enthusiastic. It's certainly fun to dress up occasionally but you'll look a trifle silly if you arrive in full fancy dress and don't know where to put your feet. *B* is a possibility, but don't get put off giving the dance a shot –

especially if you're female. An experienced tango dancer should be able to guide you across the floor with no trouble. For men it may be harder, but you've got to start somewhere after all.

If you really lack confidence a number of dance halls hold two-hour classes before the real dancing begins. Go early, learn the rudimentary steps and then dance the night away.

SITUATION SIX

You've bravely stepped out to cross *Avenida Nueve de Julio* in Buenos Aires – the world's widest road. A little green man had given you the all-clear, but at the last minute a car shoots the red light and misses you by an inch. Do you:

A Scream from the top of your voice every Argentine obscenity you know, telling him exactly what you think of his mother?

B Raise both your hands in the air in an exasperated gesture – fingers bunched together, jabbing skyward?

C Meekly retreat to the safety of the pavement and wait for the lights to change again before cautiously attempting the crossing a second time?

Comments

A will go unheard by the motorist and you'll probably just end up horrifying your fellow pedestrians with your bad language. *B* is the best response, since he'll see your sign language in his rear-view mirror (if he bothers to look), and you'll have given vent to a bit of that frustration physically. *C* is an understandable response for the pedestrian novice on Argentina's roads, but you're not going to get very far with that sort of attitude in Buenos Aires. Aggressive motorists have given rise to equally pushy pedestrians and unless you plan to confine yourself to just one half of Buenos Aires you are going to have to get used to crossing *Nueve de Julio* – all 20 lanes of it.

FURTHER READING

HISTORY: One of the best and most concise history books on Argentina is David Rock's *Argentina 1516 to 1987* (University of California Press, 1985). Alternatively try *A House Divided: Argentina 1880–1980* by Eduardo Crawley (C. Hurst and Co, 1984).

You will find no shortage of books on Juan Domingo Perón and his wife Evita. Try *Perón: A Biography* by Joseph Page (Random House, 1983) and *Evita: An Intimate Portrait of Eva Perón* by Tomás De Elia et al (Rizzoli, 1997) or the more critical *Evita: Saint or Sinner* by W.A. Harbinson (Forge, 1996). Both the semi-fictionalised *Santa Evita* (Vintage, 1997) and *The Perón Novel* (Vintage, 1999) by contemporary Argentine writer Tomás Eloy Martínez make for enjoyable reading. *Santa Evita*, especially, is a must for those who want a better understanding of Argentina's obsession with the dead. Also see V.S. Naipaul's non-fictional essay *The Return of Eva Perón* (Andre Deutsch, 1974, 1980).

The Dirty War and military dictatorships are explored in greater detail in *Argentina's Lost Patrol: Armed Struggle 1969–1979* (Yale University Press, 1995) by Maria Jose Moyano. The book is based on interviews with military and political leaders, guerrillas and journalists. Also see *A State of Fear: Memories of Argentina's Nightmare* (Eland Books, London, 1986) by Andrew Graham Yooll, editor-in-chief of the *Buenos Aires Herald*, who was forced into exile in 1976. He is also the author of *Committed Observer: Memoirs of a Journalist* (John Libby and Co, 1995).

Nunca Mas (*Never Again*) is the official report by Argentina's National Commission on Disappeared People (Faber and Faber, 1986). One of the founding mothers of the Plaza de Mayo, Matilde Mellibovsky, provides a moving account of the mothers' testimonies in *Circle of Love over Death* (Curbstone Press, Connecticut, 1997). *I Remember Julia: Voices of the Disappeared* by Eric Steiner Carlson (Temple University Press, 1996) traces the life of a disappeared doctor and mother-to-be through eyewitness accounts. The novel *Imagining Argentina* by Lawrence Thornton (Bantam, 1991) is set during the Dirty War and explores the life of a man whose wife has disappeared.

The Battle for the Falklands by Max Hastings and Simon Jenkins (W.W. Norton and Co, 1984) gives a concise account of the 1982 South Atlantic War, or try the shorter *Argentine Forces in the Falklands (Men at Arms No. 250)* by Nicholas Van Der Bijl (Osprey, 1993). Journalist Jimmy Burns, who was in Argentina during and after the Falklands War, provides an interesting account of the post-war years in *The Land that lost its Heroes: The Falklands, The Post War and Alfonsín* (Bloomsbury, 1987).

A lesser known side of Argentina's history is explored in *The Afro-Argentines of Buenos Aires, 1800–1900* by George Reid Andrews (University of Wisconsin Press, 1980). The history of the Welsh is recorded in great detail by Glyn Williams in *The Desert and the Dream: A Study of Welsh Colonisation in Chubut* (University of Wales Press, 1975). Williams also wrote *The Welsh in Patagonia* (University of Wales Press, 1991).

GAUCHOS: For everything and anything you ever wanted to know about Argentina's gauchos, don't miss *Gauchos and the Vanishing Frontier* by Richard W. Slatta (University of Nebraska Press, 1992). The epic poem *El Gaucho Martín Fierro*, written by José Hernández in the 1870s, is now considered a masterpiece and is by far the most widely read and discussed work produced in Argentina. It traces the problems faced by the gaucho, forced to yield his freedom and individuality to the social and material changes invading the pampas in the late 1800s. Bilingual editions are also available. See also *The Gaucho Martín Fierro: Adapted from the Spanish and Rendered into*

English Verse by Walter Owen. *Don Segundo Sombra* by Ricardo Güiraldes is another great gaucho classic. First published in 1926, it also laments the loss of the romantic gaucho.

TRAVEL: On a more modern-day note, Bruce Chatwin's *In Patagonia* (Penguin, 1988) is an unbeatable travel book on Patagonia and has been dubbed the book that redefined travel writing. Also see John Pilkington's *An Englishman in Patagonia* (Century, 1991) with assorted adventures including taking tea with the Welsh and discovering more about the North American bandits Butch Cassidy and the Sundance Kid, who briefly set up home in Patagonia. Their lives and South American skirmishes are explored in impeccable detail in *Digging Up Butch and Sundance* by Anne Meadows (University of Nebraska Press, 1996).

Another excellent travel book comes from Miranda France, who spent two years as a 20-something journalist in Buenos Aires. France recorded her adventures in the funny but melancholic *Bad Times in Buenos Aires* (London, Weidenfeld and Nicolson, 1998). Gerald Durrell's *The Drunken Forest* (out of print) and *The Whispering Land* (Viking, 1975) are also great travelogues.

Backpackers and the more adventurous travellers out there should get their hands on *Backpacking and Hiking in Chile and Argentina* by Tim Burford and Andrew Dixon (Bradt, 1998). And both the Lonely Planet and Footprint Handbook guides on Argentina provide good and comprehensive lists of hotels, tours and travel in Argentina. Also see the *Insight Guide on Argentina*, which has good cultural sections and fantastic colour photographs.

Charles Darwin's *The Voyage of the Beagle* (Bantam, 1972) may be quite outdated but still makes for great reading, following the naturalist in his South American travels. *Uttermost Part of the Earth* by E. Lucas Bridges (Hodder and Stoughton, 1948; Dutton, 1949) is an arresting account by the missionary Thomas Bridges' son on life growing up in Tierra del Fuego with Yamana Indians. W.H. Hudson's

Far Away and Long Ago (Lyons Press, 1997) is a book of nostalgic reminiscences of a childhood in the pampas, an absolute must for bird fans. Born in Argentina in 1841, Hudson also wrote *Idle days in Patagonia* (Chapman and Hall, 1893; Dent, 1984) and *A Naturalist in La Plata* (Dover, 1994).

NATURAL HISTORY: Birdwatchers should get their hands on *A Guide to the Birds of South America* by Rodolphe Meyer de Schauensee or *Birds of Southern South America and Antarctica (Collins Illustrated Checklist)* by Martin R. de la Pena and Maurice Rumboli (HarperCollins, 1999). *A Guide to the Birds and Mammals of Coastal Patagonia* by Graham Harris and William Conway (Princeton University Press, 1998) is also a good directory to the region's fauna.

Packed with colour photographs, William C. Leitch's *Argentine Trout Fishing: A Fly Fisherman's Guide to Patagonia* (Frank Amato, 1991) is more than just an angling guide, taking the reader on a comprehensive tour of Patagonia's rivers, streams and lakes, and giving useful practical tips.

THE LITERARY SCENE: No bibliography on Argentina would be complete without mentioning that country's greatest writers. The works of Jorge Luis Borges (1899–1986) reflect the changing character of Argentine development. Read *Labyrinths, Doctor Brodies' Report, A Universal History of Infamy, The Book of Sand* and *El Aleph*. And for a biography on the great man himself, see *Borges: A Life* by James Woodall (Basic Books, 1998). Other 20th century Argentine writers to look out for are Adolfo Bioy Casares, Tomás Eloy Martínez, Ernesto Sabato (*On Heroes and Tombs* and *El Tunel*) and Manuel Puig (*Kiss of the Spider Woman, Betrayed by Rita Hayworth, Heartbreak Tango, The Buenos Aires Affair* and *Eternal Curse on the Reader of These Pages*).

Also don't miss out on the works of one of Argentina's most famous writers, Julio Cortázar, whose works include *Los Premios*,

Rayuela (*Hopscotch*), *62*, *La Vuelta al Dia en Ochenta Mundos* and *Queremos tanto a Glenda.*

BUSINESS: Business visitors will find *Argentina Business: The portable Encyclopedia for Doing Business with Argentina* (The World Trade Press, California, 1996, 1998) indispensable. Price Waterhouse also published a booklet, *Doing Business in Argentina* (Price Waterhouse World Film Services BV, Inc, 1995). Also see *Argentina Investment & Business Guide* by Emerging Markets Investment Center (International Business Publications USA, updated annually).

BIOGRAPHIES: The rise and fall of Argentina's football star, Diego Maradona, is explored in gripping detail by Jimmy Burns in *Hand of God, The Life of Diego Maradona* (Bloomsbury, 1996). This is the unauthorised version and apparently Maradona wasn't too pleased about it.

For the definitive biography on Argentina's prodigal son, read *Che Guevara – A Revolutionary Life* by Jon Lee Anderson (London, Transworld Publishers Ltd, 1997). The early chapters also give an extraordinary insight into Argentina during the early 20th century. Guevara's own account of his motorcycle trip across South America, including Argentina, is revealed in his very own *The Motorcycle Diaries* (Verso, 1995). *The Life, Music and Times of Carlos Gardel* by Simon Collier (University of Pittsberg Press, 1986) is a good biography of Argentina's greatest tango singer. Another excellent book is *Tango!* by Simon Collier et al (Thames and Hudson, 1997).

WINE: Ending on a more bacchanalian note, *Wine Routes of Argentina* by Alan Young (International Wine Academy, 1998) is a good introduction to Argentina's burgeoning wine industry, but don't miss out on Dereck Foster's weekly wine column in the *Buenos Aires Herald* on Sundays. He also writes splendid food reviews.

ABOUT THE AUTHOR

Fiona Adams was born in London in 1973 and read Archaeology and Anthropology at Durham University. She holds a master's degree in Latin American Studies from the University of London.

It wasn't long before the English weather and a particularly vigorous travel bug drove her to the Southern Hemisphere. She taught English and History in a South African homeland for a year. Then she set her sights on South America. After an unforgettable adventure in the Amazon in 1996, there was no going back.

She has lived in South America ever since, working as a freelance journalist, dividing her time between Bolivia and Argentina, with brief forays into neighbouring Paraguay, Peru and Brazil. Always prepared to go anywhere in search of an unusual story, Adams has enjoyed such intriguing adventures as exploring the inside of Bolivia's prisons and joining an expedition in search of Atlantis.

She finally settled in Buenos Aires, seduced by the heady lifestyle of South America's most sophisticated metropolis and encouraged by her own mother who also lived in Argentina in her 20s.

INDEX

abbreviations, common, 229
accommodation, 204–8, 211
Aconcagua, Mount, 38
address, forms of, 83
addresses, 229
agriculture, 30, 39, 43, 44
AIDS, 224–5
air travel, 200–1
airport taxes, 201
airport: Ezeiza, 8, 166, 201, 237
albergue juvenil, 205
albergue transitorio, 85, 205
alfajor, 134
Alfonsín, Raúl, 29, 30, 73
Alliance Party, 28, 74
ambulance service, 225
Andes, the, 34, 37, 38, 44
animals, 209
anorexia, 62
Argentine Automobile Club (*Automovil Club Argentino*), 59, 236, 237
Argentinianisms, 181–5
argentinidad, 56, 212; *see* national identity
Argentino, Lake, 48
asado, 105, 127–9, 135, 188, 205
Austral Plan, 30
Avenida Nueve de Julio, 18, 197, 243

Bahia Blanca, 43
bakery, 136
banking, 212–13, 226
barbecue: *see asado*

bargaining, 214
Bariloche, 47, 80, 88, 98, 240
barra bravas, 162–3
beach wear, 221
beef:
    cuts, 128
    Argentine, 126–9
Bemberg, Maria Luisa, 93
bills, paying, 214
birdwatchers' guides, 247
birthday, fifteenth, 87
Boca Juniors, 148, 159–62, 164
body language, 186–7
boleadores, 21, 91
bombachas, 57, 59, 100
bombilla, 137–8
bonos, 213
bookshops, 218–20
Borges, Jorge Luis, 36, 50, 73, 156, 170, 247
bribery, 113–14
Buck, Dan, 198–200
Buenos Aires Herald, 218
Buenos Aires province, 42, 216
Buenos Aires, 8, 14, 15, 29, 34, 35–6, 80, 90, 94, 120, 121, 127, 154, 159, 181, 192–3, 195–7, 201, 203, 206, 208, 214, 216, 220–4, 229, 246
    British invasion of, 17
    Capital Federal, 19, 229
    pace of life, 36
bulimia, 63
bus guide, 237

buses, 192–3
business:
  guidebooks, 248
  networking, 110–11
  organisations, 230–1
  tips, 123–4

Cabezas, José Luis, 73
Cachi, 46
Cafayate, 46, 146
café culture, 131, 144
car:
  buying, 194–5
  hire, 194
  parking, 196–7
carbonada, 126
Carnival, 105, 241
Casa Rosada, 18, 25, 28
casinos, 43
Cassidy, Butch, 42, 198, 246
Catholicism, 149–50, 225
cattle, 15, 16, 127
cemeteries:
  Chacarita, 74, 154–5, 157
  Recoleta, 24, 25, 154–7
  undertakers, 157–8
Chaco province, 38, 44, 216
Chagas' disease, 224
Chatwin, Bruce, 20, 40, 246
Che, 84–5
children, 86–8, 115
chimichurri, 129
choripan, 135
Christmas, 113, 168
Chubut province, 38, 47, 69, 126, 216
churro, 135
cinema, 92–3
citizenship issues, 227
civil war (Unitarists vs Federalists), 19

clothes
  buying, 217
  business, 121
  see also dress code, fashion
coffee, 143–5
coimas, 113
Colón theatre, 92
Comodoro Rivadavia, 47–8
confiterías, 131, 133, 144
constitution:
  1853, 19, 28
  1994, 28
Contursi, Pascual, 102
conversation, topics of, 112, 188–9
Córdoba, 16, 17, 44, 75, 106, 108, 126,
  211, 216
Corrientes province, 38, 44, 216
Corrientes, 44
Cortázar, Julio, 73, 247
country houses, 94–5
courier companies, 215
credit cards, 212
crime, 222–3
Cuevas de las Manos, 48
currency, 30, 212–13

days of the week, 179
de la Plata, Río, 16, 17, 28, 34, 220
De la Rua, Fernando, 28, 74
debt, national, 30
democracy, 10, 28
demonstrations, 89
dengue fever, 224
desserts, 130
Diaz de Solis, Juan, 15
dieting, 62–4
dinosaurs, 40
Dirty War, the, 27, 29, 65–6, 93, 112,
  244–5

'disappeared', the, 27–8, 65–6, 73, 93, 244–5
divorce, 86
doctors, 225
dress code, 122, 220
drinks, 136; *see also* coffee, mate, wine
drivers/driving, 59–60, 192, 194–7, 222
  driving in Patagonia, 198–200
  licence, 196
  see also car
'duck', 91–2
dulce de leche, 130, 133–5

e-mail facilities, 216, 220, 235–6
economy, 29–32
  economic reforms, 30
education, 210–12
eisteddfod, 46, 51
El Calafate, 48
El Gráfico magazine, 159, 162
elections, 28, 29
electricity, 209, 216
emergencies, medical, 225
emergency telephone numbers, 229
empanada, 126, 135
employment:
  benefits, 115
  termination of, 116
energy resources, 29
Entre Ríos province, 38, 43, 216
estancias, 94, 205, 237
  famous owners, 42
European ancestry, 14
Evangelical movement, 150
Evita, the film, 24–5

facón, 57, 59, 100

facturas, 133, 180
Falkland Islands, 28, 29, 34, 74, 112, 117, 164–70, 245
Fangio, Juan Manuel, 74
farándula, 64, 158, 240
fashion, 10, 60–2, 121–2, 189, 240
  tango, 101, 220, 242
fauna, 44, 46
festivals, 47, 105–8
Fierro, Martín, 13, 74, 245
films, 93
fishing, sport, 44, 247
flag, 32
flirting, 81–2, 241
flower, national, 32
food and drink, 125–47
  immigrant influence on, 126
  ordering, 133
football, 43, 76, 159–62, 164, 188–9, 223
Formosa province, 38, 216
Frente del Pais Solidario (Frepaso), 28

Gaimán, 46, 69
Galtieri, Leopoldo, 28, 74, 78, 166–7
Garay, Juan de, 15–16, 127
Garcia, Charly, 74, 99
Gardel, Carlos, 74, 102–3, 153, 155, 183, 248
gauchada, 54
gauchos, 13, 17, 36, 56–9, 74, 245–6
  festivals, 47, 108
  games, 91–2, 127
  get-up, 57, 59, 100
  parade, 105, 106
gifts, 113
Giménez, Susana, 74
government structure, 28
graduation trip, 88

Gran Chaco, 38
Greene, Graham, 44
greeting people, 82–3, 112, 174
Guevara, Ernesto 'Che', 43, 75, 84,
    211, 248

health, 223–5
Hernández, José, 13, 74, 245
hitchhiking, 198
holiday season, 121
    bank holidays, 120
    national holidays, 18, 107–8, 115,
        166
hospitals, 225, 231–2
hotels, 204–5
housing, 205–8, 211

ice cream parlours, 217
Iguazú falls, 39, 45–6, 166
immigrants, 7–8, 15, 20, 46, 51, 69–71,
    100, 126, 129, 161, 165, 181
independence from Spain, 18, 45
Indians, 20–1
    Mapuche, 84
    Querandí, 15, 16, 21
    Tehuelche, 21, 69
    Yamana, 21, 246
inflation, 30, 32
insults, 185
Interior, the, 18–19, 35, 205, 208, 214,
    222
Internet, 216, 220, 235–6
interpreters, language, 118–19
investment, foreign, 110
invitations, 124

Jews, 51, 71, 150
Jones, Mirna, 69–70
Jujuy province, 38, 108, 213, 216

Jujuy, 16, 47, 107
juntas, military, 25–8
Justicialist Party, 22, 28

kelpers, 165, 168
kiosko, 218
kissing, 82–3

La Difunta Correa, the legend of,
    150–3
La Plata, 42
La Rioja province, 38, 76, 146, 216
La Rioja, 16, 45
labour force, 114–15
language faux pas, 180
    business, 118
Legrand, Mirtha, 75
leishmaniasis, 224
literacy, 210
locutorio, 215–16
Los Glaciares National Park, 48
Luján, 42, 149
lunfardo, 8, 102, 181

machismo, 54–6, 59
Mafalda, 76
magazines, 218
Magellan, 40
mail, 214–15
malaria, 224
Malvinas, Las Islas, 28, 29, 34, 112,
    117, 164–70
mañana syndrome, 119
manufacturing, 30
maps, 236–7
Mar del Plata, 43, 195, 203
Maradona, Diego, 54, 64, 76, 84, 103,
    158, 161, 248
market, black, 47

mate, 51, 59, 136–43
  etiquette, 140–1
  gourd, curing a, 143
  preparation, 142–3
  talk, 141–2, 188
mealtimes, 131–3
Mendoza province, 38, 146, 216
Mendoza, 44, 106
Mendoza, Pedro de, 15, 127
Menem, Carlos Saul, 28, 30, 64, 76,
  78, 117, 156, 168
Mercosur, 110
Mesopotamia, 38
metro system, *see subte*
milonga, 104, 242
Misiones province, 38, 39, 216
Mitre, Bartolomé, 19
Molinos, 46
months, 180
Monzón, Carlos, 76
Moreno glacier, 48
music, 99–100; *see also* tango

Nahuel Huapí, Lake, 47
names, 190
national identity, 56
nepotism, 111
Neuquén province, 38, 216
newspapers, 218, 220
nicknames, 83–5, 133
numbers, 123, 178–9

Pachamama, 150
Paez, Fito, 76, 99
Pago Facil, 214
pampas, 16, 29, 33, 34, 37–8, 127,
  205, 247
panadería, 136
pancho, 135

Paraná, 43
Paraná, Río, 38, 43, 44, 136
parrilla, 127–9, 213
parrillada, 129
paseo, el, 89
Pastorutti, Soledad, 99
pastries, 133
Patagonia, 40–2, 69, 127, 198–200,
  205, 221, 224, 246, 247
pato, 91–2
Patoruzú, 77
pedestrians, 197–8, 222, 243
Península Valdés, 46
Perón, Eva 'Evita', 22–5, 77, 153,
  156–7, 244
Perón, Juan Domingo, 22–3, 25, 30,
  73, 77, 157, 201, 244
peronistas/peronismo, 22–5, 28, 76,
  77, 156, 157, 189
personal space, 124
petroleum, 43, 47
pets, 209
pharmacy, 217, 231
Piazzolla, Astor, 77
picada, 135
piropos, 56, 117, 187–8
plastic surgery, 64
Plaza de Mayo, mothers and
  grandmothers of the, 65–7, 244–5
police, 72
political parties, 22, 28–9
pollution, 35, 223
polo, 95–8, 238
Popham, Home, 17
porteños, 14, 17, 18, 35–6, 48, 54, 67,
  77, 81, 94, 102, 126, 173, 192, 193,
  205, 209, 220
  in relation to other Argentines,
  18–19

post office, 214–15
prehistoric caves, 48
privatisation, 30, 76, 110, 114, 201
Proceso, El, 27, 65, 73, 74, 78, 93
propinas, 113–14
Protestants, 150
provinces, 34
provoletta, 129
psychoanalysis, 67–9
Puenzo, Luis, 93
Puerto Madryn, 46
punctuality, 119

Quilmes, 45
quincena, 87
Quino, 76
quintas, 94
Quinterno, Dante, 77

Radical Party, 29, 73
rastra, 59, 100
recycling, 209
red tide, 130, 223
religion, indigenous, 150; *see also*
  Catholicism, Jews
remise, 194, 201
Resistencia, 44
restaurants:
  parrilla, 128
  tenador libre, 134
  words to say, 176
Río Gallegos, 48, 216
Río Negro province, 38, 146, 216
River Plate, 159, 161–2, 164
rodeo, 92, 106
Rosario, 43, 75
Rosas, Juan Manuel de, 19, 93, 156
Route 2, 203
Route 40, 38, 199

Sabatini, Gabriela, 77
Salta province, 38, 146, 213, 216
Salta, 16, 47, 107, 202
San Juan province, 38, 146, 150, 153,
  216
San Juan, 45, 108
San Martín, José de, 18, 107, 153
Santa Cruz province, 38, 48, 216
schools, 210–12
  bilingual, 212, 232–3
seafood, 130
seatbelts, 60, 195, 222
secretaries, 117, 119
security guards, 72
shopping, 216–20
  food, 135–6
  words to say, 176–7
siesta, 120, 222
skiing, 98–9, 220, 240
slang, 181–5; *see also lunfardo*
smoking, 124
snacks, 134–5
sobremesa, 134
Solanas, Fernando, 93
Sosa, Mercedes, 34, 77, 99
South Atlantic War, 166–70, 245
Spanish conquest, 15
Spanish language:
  courses, 234–5
  pronunciation, 172–3
  see also lunfardo
subte, el, 203–4
Sundance Kid, 42, 198, 246

tango, 8, 9, 74, 77, 79, 93, 100–5, 137,
  181, 183, 220, 238, 242–3, 248
taxes, 122–3, 226
  tax haven, 49

taxis, 193–4
taxi drivers, 8, 10, 194, 214
teahouses, Welsh, 46
telephone system, 215–16, 228–9
television, 220
theatre, 92, 220
Tierra del Fuego, 7, 18, 34, 37, 49, 130, 203, 210, 216, 221, 246
time:
telling, 178
timekeeping, 80, 85, 119–21, 124, 221–2
Tinelli, Marcelo, 77
tipping, 113, 134, 136, 213–14
titles, 83
tourist card, 226
tourist offices, 237
trade unions, 30, 115–16
train travel, 201–4
trasnochador, 81
truco, 89–91, 187
Tucumán, 16, 18, 45, 203, 205, 213, 216

unemployment, 30, 32, 114
Unión Cívica Radical (UCR), 28
universities, 44, 211–12, 235
Ushuaia, 37, 49, 98, 150
usted, use of, 83, 174

vacation, paid, 115
vaccinations, 225
Vallecito, 150–2

vegetarians, 126
Videla, Jorge Rafael, 25, 29, 78
Viedma, 35
villas miserias, 71–2, 208, 209
vineyards, 44, 45, 46, 146–7
Viola, Roberto, 78
Virgin of Luján, 42, 78, 149
visa:
business, 122, 226
exemptions, 226
student, 212
viveza criolla, 54, 91, 192
vivos, 54, 77
vos, use of, 83, 174
voseo, 174

wages, 115
waiters, 133–4
weddings, 85
weekends, 80
Welsh immigrants, 46, 51, 69–70, 126, 245, 246
wine, 145–7, 248
women, 60–2
nicknames for, 85
trophy wives, 117
workers, 116–17

Yabrán, Alfredo, 73
yerba mate, 57, 136, 218, 239–40; *see mate*
youth hostels, 204–5